Easy Windows NT®
Workstation 4.0

by Nancy Price Warner
and Scott L. Warner

Easy Windows NT Workstation 4.0

Copyright© 1997 Que® Corporation

All rights reserved. No part of this book shall be reproduced, stored in a retrieval system, or transmitted by any means, electronic, mechanical, photocopying, recording, or otherwise, without written permission from the publisher. No patent liability is assumed with respect to the use of the information contained herein. While every precaution has been taken in the preparation of this book, the publisher and author assume no responsibility for errors or omissions. Neither is any liability assumed for damages resulting from the use of the information contained herein. For information, address Que Corporation, 201 West 103rd Street, Indianapolis, IN 46290. You can reach Que's direct sales line by calling 1-800-428-5331.

Library of Congress Catalog Card Number: 97-65010

International Standard Book Number: 0-7897-1164-8

99   98   97   8   7   6   5   4   3   2   1

Interpretation of the printing code: the rightmost double-digit number is the year of the book's first printing; the rightmost single-digit number is the number of the book's printing. For example, a printing code of 97-1 shows that this copy of the book was printed during the first printing of the book in 1997.

Screen reproductions in this book were created by means of the program Collage Complete from Inner Media, Inc, Hollis, NH.

Printed in the United States of America

Dedication

We would like to dedicate this book to each other. Our first book together, and hopefully not our last.

Credits

Publisher
Roland Elgey

Publishing Manager
Lynn E. Zingraf

Editorial Services Director
Elizabeth Keaffaber

Managing Editor
Michael Cunningham

Director of Marketing
Lynn E. Zingraf

Acquisitions Editor
Martha O'Sullivan

Technical Specialist
Nadeem Muhammed

Product Development Specialist
Henly Wolin

Technical Editors
Bill Bruns
Keith Whitemore

Production Editor
Katie Purdum

Book Designers
Barbara Kordesh
Ruth Harvey

Cover Designers
Dan Armstrong
Kim Scott

Production Team
Erin M. Danielson, Trey Frank,
Amy Gornik, Tim Neville,
Kaylene Riemen, Julie Searls,
Sossity Smith, Paul Wilson

Indexer
Kevin Fulcher

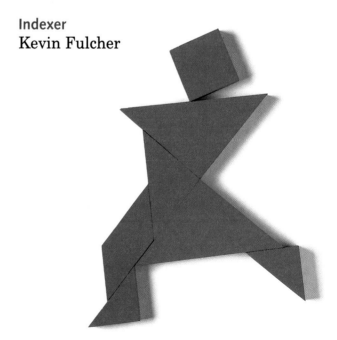

Composed in *Syntax* and *New Century Schoolbook* by Que Corporation.

About the Authors

Scott and **Nancy Warner** are private consultants in the Computer and Publishing arenas. They have BS degrees in Computer Information Systems from Purdue University. Scott has written or contributed to many books for Que; Nancy used to be a Product Director and Marketing Manager for Macmillan Computer Publishing. Visit their Web site at **www.infinet-is.com/~warner** for more
information.

Acknowledgments

I would like to thank my mother (Pauline) and my father (John) for being such wonderful influences in my life. You taught me to love to learn and always strive for what I want. In addition, I would like to thank my sister (Julie) for always being there—you have so much courage and class—I learn so much from you.
—Nancy

I would like to thank Rhonda & Pat, Sandy & Mike, Mary Jo & Tim, Ronald Allen & Delaine, for all your support and encouragement while I was growing up. By the way, I like mustard now.
—Scott

We would both like to thank the people at Que who helped make this a successful project. Martha O'Sullivan, Katie Purdum, and Henly Wolin—you guys were great to work with! We also want to mention Lorna Gentry, Caroline Roop, and Joe Wikert, just because we like them.

We would also like to thank Joan Goldstein—without you, we wouldn't have studied computer information systems, met each other, and lived happily ever after.

Trademarks

All terms mentioned in this book that are known to be trademarks or service marks have been appropriately capitalized. Que Corporation cannot attest to the accuracy of this information. Use of a term in this book should not be regarded as affecting the validity of any trademark or service mark.

We'd Like to Hear from You!

As part of our continuing effort to produce books of the highest possible quality, Que would like to hear your comments. To stay competitive, we *really* want you, as a computer book reader and user, to let us know what you like or dislike most about this book or other Que products.

You can mail comments, ideas, or suggestions for improving future editions to the address below, or send us a fax at (317) 581-4663. For the online inclined, Macmillan Computer Publishing has a forum on CompuServe (type **GO QUEBOOKS** at any prompt) through which our staff and authors are available for questions and comments. The address of our Internet site is **http://www.quecorp.com** (World Wide Web).

In addition to exploring our forum, please feel free to contact me personally to discuss your opinions of this book: I'm **hwolin@aol.com** on America Online, and I'm **hwolin@que.mcp.com** on the Internet.

Although we cannot provide general technical support, we're happy to help you resolve problems you encounter related to our books, disks, or other products. If you need such assistance, please contact our Tech Support department at 800-545-5914 ext. 3833.

To order other Que or Macmillan Computer Publishing books or products, please call our Customer Service department at 800-835-3202 ext. 666.

Thanks in advance—your comments will help us to continue publishing the best books available on computer topics in today's market.

Henly Wolin
Product Development Specialist
Que Corporation
201 W. 103rd Street
Indianapolis, Indiana 46290
USA

Contents

Contents

Introduction

Windows NT has so many helpful features that whether you are a beginning user or an advanced user, you can benefit from its capabilities. Using Windows NT, you can open applications from the Start menu or by using Shortcuts. You can switch between applications by clicking the taskbar or the window title bar. Windows NT encourages you to share information between applications, rather than typing things repetitively. Find folders and files with a few clicks, get help, or manage your hard disk with Windows NT Explorer. You can even set up immediate access to the Internet and the option to send electronic mail or faxes. Windows NT allows you to secure your files as well as play games. And if you forget to back up your hard disk regularly, you can simply set Windows NT to backup automatically.

Windows NT is an operating system that utilizes a graphical environment. This is why you have a desktop, instead of a command prompt. Additionally, Windows NT lets you accomplish several tasks at the same time. For instance, you can print from Excel, while you are setting up a fax in Word, all while you are searching for a file. And not only that, if you are connected to a network, you can share resources. Some of the resources you can share are printers, other people's computers, and files on a server. All these things make your job easier and more efficient.

Specifically, you can use Windows NT to accomplish the following:

- *Start Windows NT*. Logging in and out of the computer will become second nature to you, once you learn how. Then, with the use of the mouse and the Start button, you are ready to tackle Windows NT.

- *Manipulating windows and your desktop*. Windows NT displays all of its information in on-screen boxes called *windows*. It is very important to understand how these windows work so that you can become familiar with maneuvering your desktop.

- *Managing your folders and files*. You can open and close folders to view their contents, or you can create new folders to keep your saved information organized. In addition to creating new folders, you can copy or move an old folder to a new location. All of these things you can do with separate windows, or through the Windows NT Explorer.

- *Control your applications*. One of the biggest advantages of using Windows NT is the control it gives you over your applications. Windows NT applications are easy to open and use. You can add shortcuts to your desktop or rearrange your menus for quick access to applications.

- *Print from Windows NT*. Print documents from Windows NT applications and use the print queue to pause, restart, or cancel print jobs. You can add a printer to the setup, change settings and properties, and select a default printer of your choice.

- *Share information and resources*. You can easily share and link data between applications. Windows NT makes shared files easy to access over a network. In addition to files, you can share resources like printers and other computers.

- *Utilize the Internet*. If you have a modem or a network connection to the Internet, you can send electronic mail, receive electronic mail, or even browse the World Wide Web.

- *Use Windows NT accessories*. Windows NT provides many applications that you can use to help you in your work, be creative, or have fun. A few of these applications are Paint, multimedia tools, WordPad, Microsoft Fax, and games like Solitaire, 3-D PinBall, Minesweeper, or FreeCell.

- *Maintain your system*. Back up your hard disk automatically, secure your files, or even monitor your computer's performance with Windows NT.

- *Personalize Windows NT*. There are many ways you can customize Windows NT. By customizing your desktop colors, settings, or other Windows NT features, you can make your work more enjoyable as well as efficient.

Task Sections

The Task sections include numbered steps that tell you how to accomplish certain tasks such as saving a workbook or filling a range. The numbered steps walk you through a specific example so that you can learn the task by doing it.

Big Screen

At the beginning of each task is a large screen that shows how the computer screen will look after you complete the procedure that follows in that task. Sometimes the screen shows a feature discussed in that task, however, such as a shortcut menu.

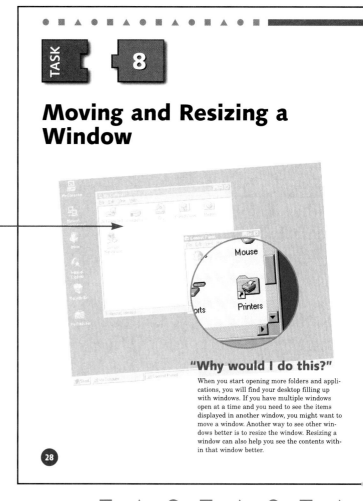

TASK

8

Moving and Resizing a Window

"Why would I do this?"

When you start opening more folders and applications, you will find your desktop filling up with windows. If you have multiple windows open at a time and you need to see the items displayed in another window, you might want to move a window. Another way to see other windows better is to resize the window. Resizing a window can also help you see the contents within that window better.

28

Step-by-Step Screens

Each task includes a screen shot for each step of a procedure that shows how the computer screen will look at each step in the process.

Task 8: Moving and Resizing a Window

1 To move an open window, point anywhere on the title bar, and then click and drag the window to your desired position on the desktop. Notice that the entire contents of the selected window move with your mouse pointer. Try moving the Control Panel window.

Puzzled?

Click and drag will always refer to clicking the left mouse button, holding the button down, and dragging the window. If you are having problems with this, please refer back to Task 2, "Using the Mouse."

2 Position the mouse pointer over any one window border (try the right side) until a double-headed arrow appears. Click and drag the border toward the left of the window to reduce the size, or to the right to increase the size. You can also click and drag the corners of a window to resize both dimensions at one time.

3 If the window is too small to show all its contents, horizontal and/or vertical scroll bars appear. Click the arrow at either end of a scroll bar to view the hidden contents of the window. ■

Missing Link

You can scroll a little at a time by manipulating the scroll arrows. You can click and drag the actual scroll bar. Or, you can scroll in jumps by clicking in the scroll bar area between the bar and the arrow. You can also switch from one window to another by pressing the **Alt** or **Tab** keys simultaneously.

29

Puzzled? Notes

You may find that you performed a task, such as sorting data, that you didn't want to do after all.

Missing Link

Many tasks contain other short notes that tell you a little more about certain procedures. These notes define terms, explain other options, refer you to other sections when applicable, and so on.

PART I

Getting Started with Windows NT

1 Logging On

2 Using the Mouse

3 Using the Start Button

4 Locking and Logging Off

5 Shutting Down the Computer

To start Windows NT Workstation, turn on your computer and monitor. Depending on how your computer is *configured*, you might be asked to select an operating system. This will happen if your computer is set up for a dual boot. A dual boot is a setup option that allows you to use either the Windows NT Workstation operating system or another operating system like Windows 95, DOS, or OS/2 to run your computer. Press the up or down arrow on the keyboard to select the operating system, then press the Enter key to confirm your choice.

Choose Windows NT Workstation. If you only have Windows NT on your computer, you do not have to select anything. The default Windows NT operating system will start automatically.

The computer will run through its general start-up procedures and then display the Windows NT Workstation Welcome screen. Once the logon screen appears, you will need to log on to Windows NT to access your desktop.

Your desktop is the area on-screen that displays icons and windows. From the desktop, you can open and switch between applications, search for specific folders, print documents, and perform other tasks. The following list explains the components of the desktop:

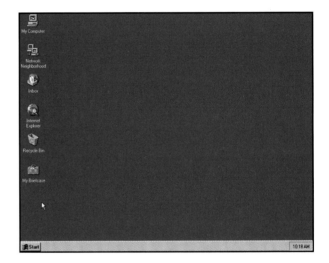

- **My Computer** contains your computer's drives and directories, the Control Panel, Dial-up Networking, and the Printers folder. You will learn how to manipulate the My Computer window in this part. Part IV explains how to use the My Computer window to manage your files.

- The **Network Neighborhood** displays shared resources on a network.

- The **Recycle Bin** is where deleted files (not from a command prompt or network drive) are placed until you select them to be removed permanently. If you change your mind about removing a file, you can restore it from the recycle bin.

- **My Briefcase** is used to synchronize files you use on multiple Windows computers (for instance your laptop and desktop computers).

- The **Inbox** is an icon representing Microsoft Exchange that enables you to send and receive faxes and electronic mail messages.

- The **taskbar** is a horizontal bar located along the bottom of the screen that displays the Start button and any open applications or folders. You can show or hide the taskbar, and you can even move it from its original location to make your work easier. Part II explains how to perform these tasks.

- The **Start** button provides a menu offering quick access to programs, documents, settings, help topics, and more.

- You will also see **windows** on the desktop. They are rectangular areas on-screen containing folders, files, documents, dialog boxes, messages, and more. You can easily move, size, and manipulate the windows to organize your desktop to suit your working routine. You open windows to view and make use of the items and applications within them.

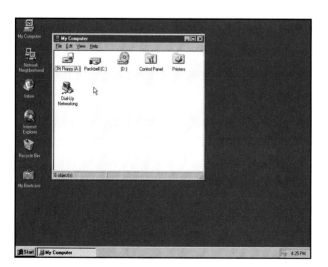

The best way to maneuver around the desktop is by using your mouse. Part I gives you some practice using your mouse on the desktop.

When you finish working in NT, you should either log off of NT, lock Windows NT, or shut down the computer. If you are not finished with your computer, but are leaving briefly (for example, going to a meeting), you may want to lock your computer so others cannot access your files and information. Locking the workstation allows you to leave the computer and keep others from compromising your security. If you share your computer with others, you may need to leave your computer on after you've finished working; in that case, you need to log off of Windows NT. Logging off ensures that your files and data are secure, but enables you to leave the computer on so that others can access your computer's resources.

If you want to turn the computer off entirely when you've finished working in NT, before you flip the computer switch to off, you must shut it down properly. If you turn off the computer without first shutting it down, you may lose unsaved data or files. It is also important to know that shutting down your computer automatically logs you off of Windows NT.

Whether you want to log on, lock, log off, maneuver the mouse, use the Start button, or shut down the computer, the tasks that follow will give you the basic information you will need to get started in Windows NT.

Logging On

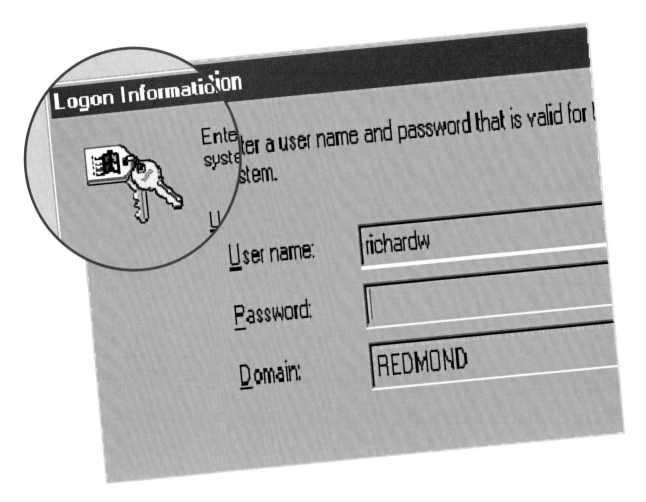

"Why would I do this?"

Whether you just turned your computer on or you are going to start a new session of Windows NT, you will need to log on. Logging on allows you access to your applications, folders, and files. This task teaches you the correct way to log on to Windows NT.

1 Turn on the computer and wait for the Begin Logon dialog box to appear. Depending on your hardware and configuration, there might be a wait while your computer starts up. There might even be a dual boot screen, as discussed earlier. After Windows NT begins, a dialog box will appear and ask you to press the **Ctrl+Alt+Delete** keys at the same time. Ctrl+Alt+Del in Windows NT Workstation allows you to choose specific functions that are associated with the Once you do this, the Logon Information dialog box appears.

2 Type your **User name** and **Password** into the text boxes, then press **Enter** on the keyboard, or click the **OK** button. Your user name should have been assigned to you when you or your administrator installed Windows NT.

Missing Link

Make sure you enter your user name and password using the correct case. Windows NT distinguishes between upper- and lowercase. If you enter in the wrong password, there will be a Logon Message dialog box that tells you to press **Enter** and type the correct password.

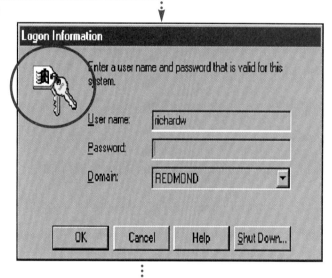

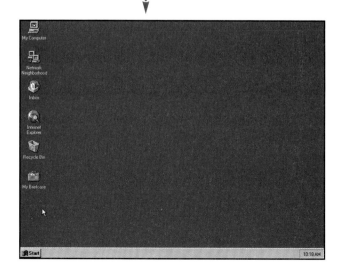

3 The desktop will be displayed and you are officially logged in to Windows NT. ■

TASK 2

Using the Mouse

"Why would I do this?"

The mouse is used to manipulate objects on the Windows NT desktop. While most of the functions performed with the mouse can be accomplished using the keyboard, it is usually easier and quicker to use the mouse. When you move the mouse on the mousepad, the on-screen pointer (arrow) moves accordingly. You point to things on the screen and press the buttons on the mouse to let the computer know what you want to do.

The mouse usually has two buttons, referred to as the "left" and "right" mouse buttons. (Task

73, "Adjusting the Mouse," will show you how to alter mouse options. For example, if you are left-handed, you can set up the mouse to accommodate you better.) As you learn in this book, clicking each button accomplishes specific tasks. Practice moving the mouse around so that you get used to moving it up, down, left, right, and diagonally. This task will show you how to manipulate different Windows NT elements on your desktop with your mouse. Also, use the table at the end of the task as a mouse refresher course.

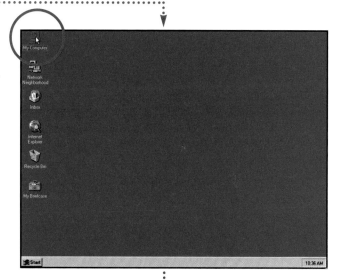

1 Move the mouse, and you will see that the arrow moves around the screen. You use the mouse to position your cursor, and to select and move items on your computer screen.

Missing Link

When I ask you to click, I am referring to the left mouse button. If you need to use the right mouse button, I will specify for you to right-click. If you are left-handed and you reversed the mouse buttons for Windows NT, simply choose the opposite button.

2 To select an icon, position the mouse so that the pointer is over the item. For example, to select the **My Computer** icon move your pointer to rest on the icon, then click once with the left mouse button. When you have clicked the icon, it is highlighted to indicate it has been selected.

Puzzled?

Make sure you do not click the words below the icon; this is the icon or filename. If you click the file name, you can click once somewhere else on the desktop and try clicking the icon again.

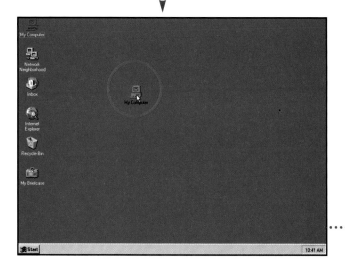

3 To select and drag an item, press the left mouse button and hold it down. While you hold the button down, move the mouse to a new position on the desktop. As you drag the item, you can see a "ghost" that moves with your pointer. When you release the mouse button, the item stays in its new location.

Task 2: Using the Mouse

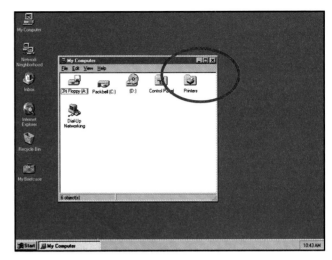

4 Point to the **My Computer** icon and double click the left mouse button. Double-
clicking can be described as clicking the
mouse button twice in rapid succession
without moving the mouse. When you
double-click items, Windows NT opens that
window, program, drive, or document. To
close the window, click the **Close** button
(X) in the top right corner of the window. ■

Mouse Moves Review

Move	What Happens as a Result...
Point	Move your mouse so the corresponding on-screen pointer touches the item you want to select.
Click	Press and release the left mouse button after positioning the on-screen mouse pointer.
Drag	Hold down the left mouse button and move the mouse across your desk until the on-screen pointer and the selected item are in the position you want. Then release the mouse button.
Double-click	Click the mouse button twice in rapid succession without moving the mouse.

Using the Start Button

"Why would I do this?"

The taskbar, the gray horizontal bar along the bottom of the screen, has a Start Button on the far left side. This Start button enables you to start applications, open documents, customize Windows NT settings, get Help, find items, and more.

Task 3: Using the Start Button

1 Point to the **Start** button on the left side of the taskbar with the mouse and click the left mouse button. The Start menu appears.

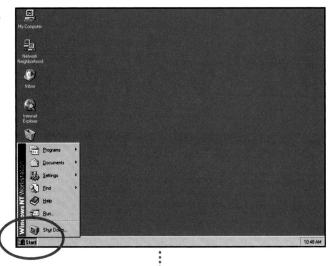

Missing Link

When your pointer is on the Start button, you might see a pop-up bubble—called a ToolTip—that displays **Click here to begin**. ToolTips are part of Windows NT Help. When your pointer rests over a button momentarily, the ToolTip tells you what that button is for. This can be handy if you cannot remember which button you need.

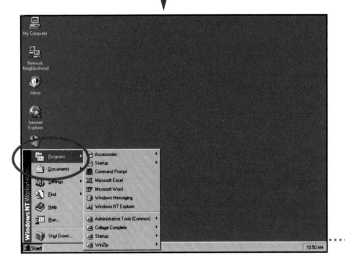

2 Move the mouse pointer to the **Program** command on the menu to display a secondary menu of items; for example, the Accessories and Startup folders appear on the Program menu. In addition, applications installed on your computer might have commands on the Programs menu.

3 Point the mouse pointer at the **Accessories** folder on the **Start** menu to display a submenu of programs in the folder. If you wanted one of the items in the Accessories submenu, you would point to the item's name and click. For now, click somewhere on the desktop to close the Start menu. ■

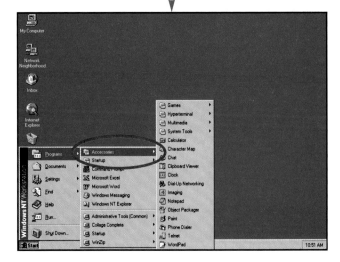

Locking and Logging Off

"Why would I do this?"

If you are going to be away from your computer for a short period of time (weekly meeting), but do not want to compromise the security of your files, there is an alternative to logging off Windows NT or shutting down the computer. You can lock your workstation so that no one can access your computer or any of its files unless they have your Windows NT User name and Password. On the other hand, if you share a computer with a coworker, each of you will have your own user name. Occasionally you may

need to log off NT to allow your coworker to log on. Also, if your workstation has resources that are shared by other users on your network, you may need to log off rather than shut down your computer when you've finished working in NT. Logging off allows others to access your workstation's resources in your absence; shutting down the computer makes these resources unreachable by anyone. This task describes how to correctly lock your computer and log off Windows NT.

Task 4: Locking and Logging Off

1 Locking the workstation is a very simple step. Press the **Ctrl+Alt+Del** keys simultaneously and a Windows NT Security dialog box will appear. There will be six buttons for you to choose from. To lock the workstation, choose the **Lock Workstation** button.

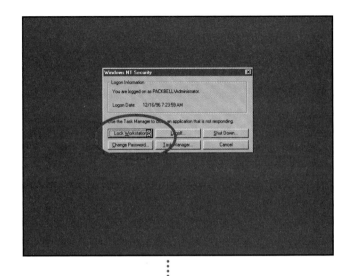

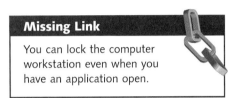

Missing Link

You can lock the computer workstation even when you have an application open.

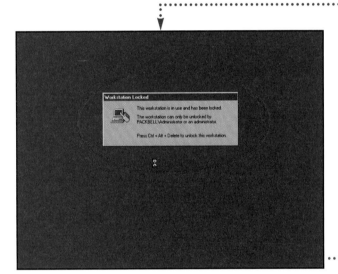

2 A **Workstation Locked** message box will appear. It explains that the workstation has been locked and can only be unlocked by the current user or administrator. When you return to unlock your workstation and start using your computer again, you must press the **Ctrl+Alt+Del** keys.

3 This will give you the **Unlock Workstation** dialog box, similar to the logon dialog box. It will ask you for the **Password** to that workstation's current User name. Enter the correct User name and choose the **OK** button. Your desktop will be exactly where you left it.

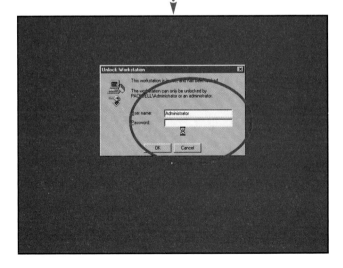

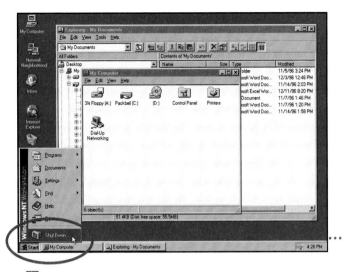

4 When you would rather log off the computer while you attend your meeting, follow these steps. Before logging off the computer, you can choose to close all open programs, open windows, and folders; though it is not necessary. Open the **Start** menu and click **Shut Down**.

5 Windows NT checks the system and prepares for the shut down. You can tell this because the desktop area darkens and the **Shut Down Windows** dialog box appears. The dialog box asks you whether you want to shut down the computer, restart the computer, or close all programs and log on as a different user.

> **Missing Link**
>
> Another way to log off the workstation is to press the **Ctrl+Alt+Del** keys simultaneously. When the dialog box appears, choose the **Logoff** button.

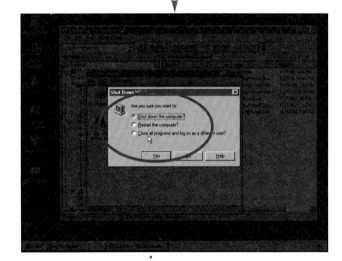

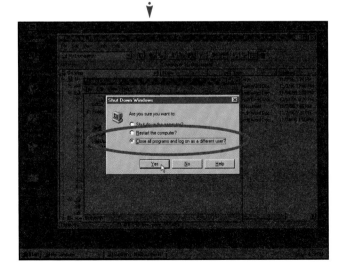

6 Click the **Close all programs and log on as a different user?** radio button and click the **Yes** button to complete the task. If you have any unsaved work, Windows NT will have the program automatically prompt you to save the work. The current session will be ended and another user may log in using the method described in Task 1. ■

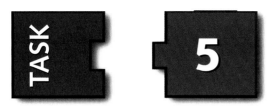

TASK

5

Shutting Down the Computer

"Why would I do this?"

If you turn the power to your computer off before you shut it down, you could lose valuable data or damage an open file. Windows NT provides a safe Shut Down feature that checks for open programs and files, warns you to save unsaved files, and prepares for you to turn off your computer.

1 Open the **Start** menu and click **Shut Down**. Windows NT checks the system and prepares for the shut down. You can tell this because the desktop area darkens. The **Shut Down Windows** dialog box appears and asks you what you want to do.

2 The default selection in the Shut Down Window dialog box is **Shut down the Computer?** If another option is selected, click the **Shut Down the Computer?** radio button and click the **Yes** button to complete the task. Windows NT displays a final screen that tells you it is safe to turn off your computer.

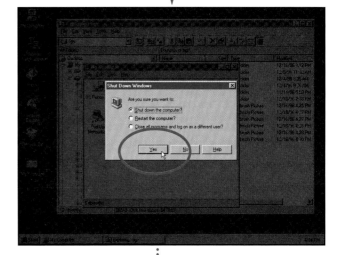

Missing Link

It is important to note that when you shut down the computer properly, it automatically logs you off. This means Task 4, "Locking and Logging Off," would not be necessary.

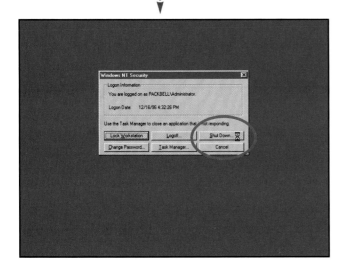

3 Another way to shut down the workstation is to press the **Ctrl+Alt+Del** keys simultaneously. When the **Windows NT Security** dialog box appears, choose the **Shut Down...** button. A final Shutdown Computer dialog box will appear asking you whether you want to Shut down the computer or Shut down and Restart the computer. Select the **Shutdown** radio button and choose the **OK** button. The computer will safely shut down. ■

PART II

Working with Windows

WINDOWS NT DISPLAYS all of its information in on-screen boxes called *windows*. It is very important to understand how these windows work so that you can become familiar with maneuvering your desktop.

When you have windows open, you can maximize the space on your desktop by reducing or enlarging a window. You may need to completely move a window in order to see another window in the background. When you have finished with a window, you can close it in many different ways.

The menus that are associated with each window are similar. They get more complicated once you start working with applications. These menus can help you view, copy, and delete information in a window, and accomplish many more tasks.

We will talk about dialog boxes and how you use their common elements. Dialog boxes contain options that will allow you to control windows, applications, and documents. This will become more important as we move throughout this book. Dialog boxes are everywhere in Windows NT.

You can change the way each window is displayed and then rearrange them on the desktop. You can even close them in different ways, either for good, or to quickly open a window again. This will be very handy when you start doing multiple tasks at the same time.

You will find that throughout these tasks there is more than one way to complete the task. Just remember that this book will teach you the easiest way to complete the task. In the special notes provided we will try to give you alternatives so that you can decide what is most comfortable to you.

Opening a Window

"Why would I do this?"

Before you work with any of the information on your computer, you must know how to display these windows. If you want to look in a window to see what folders or files are stored there, you can open the window.

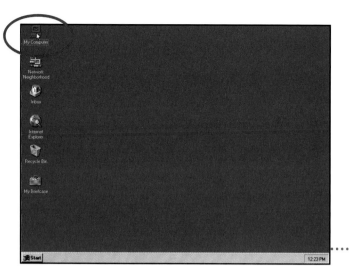

1 Point to the **My Computer** icon with the mouse pointer. Double-click the left mouse button to display the contents of the window.

2 A window and its contents open up. You know it is the **My Computer** window because the name is located in the title bar.

Missing Link

The title bar contains the Control menu icon (in the upper-left corner) and the window title (**My Computer**), along with three buttons on the right. We will talk more about the title bar in Tasks 7 and 12.

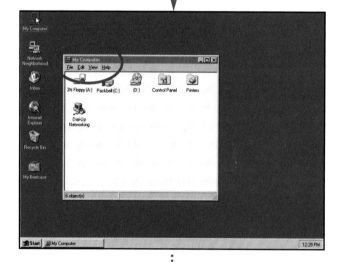

3 Point to the **Control Panel** icon inside the My Computer window. Click the right mouse button to display the icon's shortcut menu. Then click the word **Open** with the left mouse button to choose that command.

Missing Link

Shortcut menus offer commands related to the object you right-click. Try right-clicking the mouse on the taskbar or on the desktop to see the shortcut menus.

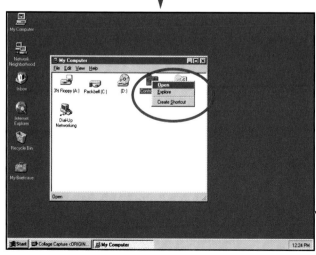

23

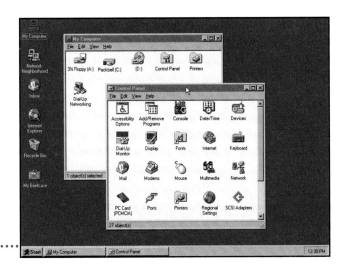

4 The Control Panel window opens and displays the contents of the window.

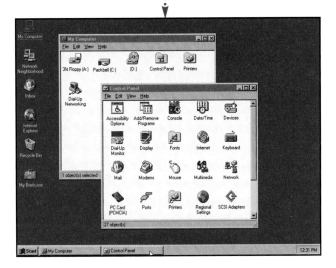

5 Notice that buttons for the My Computer and the Control Panel windows appear on the taskbar next to the Start Button. ▪

Puzzled?

Notice that the Control Panel button on the taskbar looks as if it is depressed. This is because it is the *active* window, or the window that you are currently using. In addition, the active window's title bar is a more prominent color.

Minimizing and Maximizing a Window

"Why would I do this?"

There will be times when you need to reduce or enlarge program and document windows to make your work easier. You might want to reduce a window if you are not going to use it for a while, but want to be able to access it from the taskbar. If you are going to be working in a specific application, like Paint, you might want to enlarge the window so that it covers the entire desktop.

Task 7: Minimizing and Maximizing a Window

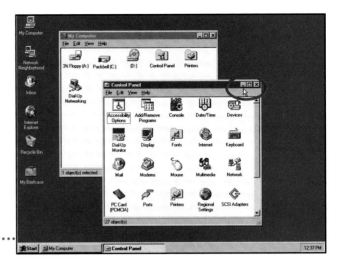

1 You should have the My Computer and the Control Panel windows open on your desktop. The Control Panel window should be the active window. If it is not, click somewhere in the **Control Panel** window. Point the mouse at the **Minimize** button. Click the left mouse button. This window is no longer on the desktop; it is now a button on the taskbar.

2 Point at the **Control Panel** button on the taskbar with the mouse pointer and click with the left mouse button. The Control Panel window will open back up to the shape it was before.

Missing Link

Almost all application and document windows have Minimize and Maximize buttons. They also have a Control menu icon that contains commands related to the open window. Access this menu by clicking the left-most icon in the title bar, or by right-clicking anywhere on the title bar.

3 Point the mouse at the **Maximize** button— the button in the upper right corner that contains a rectangle—and click the left-mouse button. This window enlarges to take up the entire screen, and the Maximize button has changed to the Restore button, which looks like two rectangles.

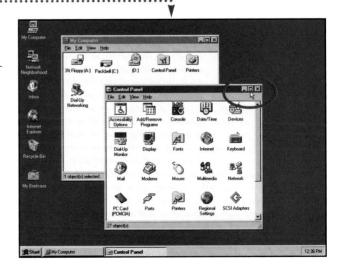

4 Click the **Restore** button to change the Control Panel window back to the size you started out with. ■

Missing Link

An alternative to clicking the Maximize and Restore buttons is double-clicking the window title bar.

Window Size Icons

Click This Button	To
▬	Reduce a window to a button on the taskbar.
◻	Enlarge a window so that it fills the entire screen.
⧉	Return a window to its normal size.

Moving and Resizing a Window

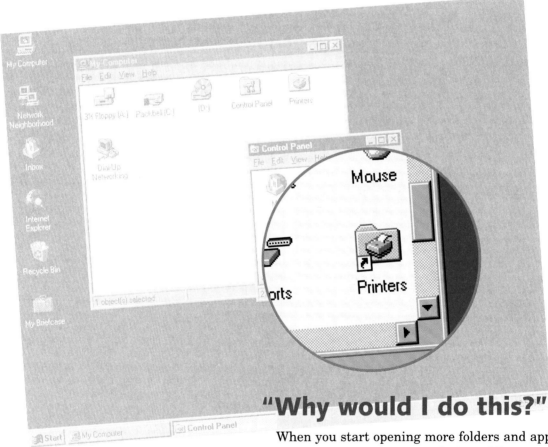

"Why would I do this?"

When you start opening more folders and applications, you will find your desktop filling up with windows. If you have multiple windows open at a time and you need to see the items displayed in another window, you might want to move a window. Another way to see other windows better is to resize the window. Resizing a window can also help you see the contents within that window better.

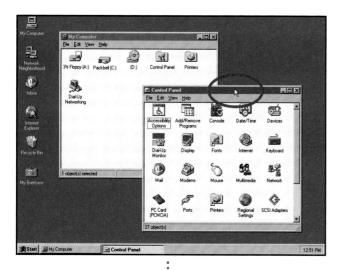

1 To move an open window, point anywhere on the title bar, and then click and drag the window to your desired position on the desktop. Notice that the entire contents of the selected window move with your mouse pointer. Try moving the Control Panel window.

Puzzled?

Click and drag will always refer to clicking the left mouse button, holding the button down, and dragging the window. If you are having problems with this, please refer back to Task 2, "Using the Mouse."

2 Position the mouse pointer over any one window border (try the right side) until a double-headed arrow appears. Click and drag the border toward the left of the window to reduce the size, or to the right to increase the size. You can also click and drag the corners of a window to resize both dimensions at one time.

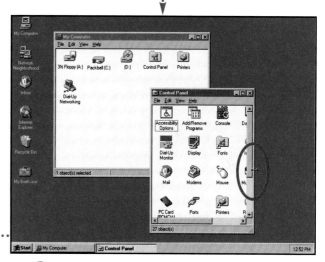

3 If the window is too small to show all its contents, horizontal and/or vertical scroll bars appear. Click the arrow at either end of a scroll bar to view the hidden contents of the window. ■

Missing Link

You can scroll a little at a time by manipulating the scroll arrows. You can click and drag the actual scroll bar. Or, you can scroll in jumps by clicking in the scroll bar area between the bar and the arrow. You can also switch from one window to another by pressing the **Alt** or **Tab** keys simultaneously.

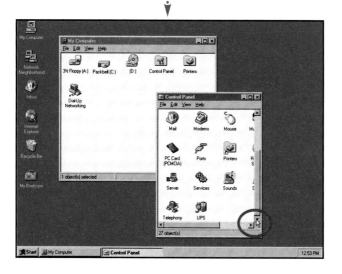

Closing Windows

"Why would I do this?"

Now that you have learned the many things you can do with windows, you are going to learn to close them. If you are finished with a window and you want to remove it from your desktop, you will close the folder.

1 You can close a window by clicking the **Close** button (**X**) on the right corner of the window's title bar. Try closing the Control Panel window.

2 You can close a window by clicking once on the **Control** menu box in the left corner of the title bar. Choose the **Close** command. Try closing the My Computer window. ■

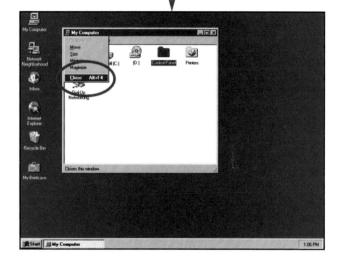

Puzzled?

Step 1 is the most efficient way to close a window—but there are other ways. You can select a window, then press **Alt+F4**. Or, double-click the **Control** menu icon. Or, if the window has a menu, you can close it by opening the **File** menu and then choosing the **Close** command.

10

Using Menus

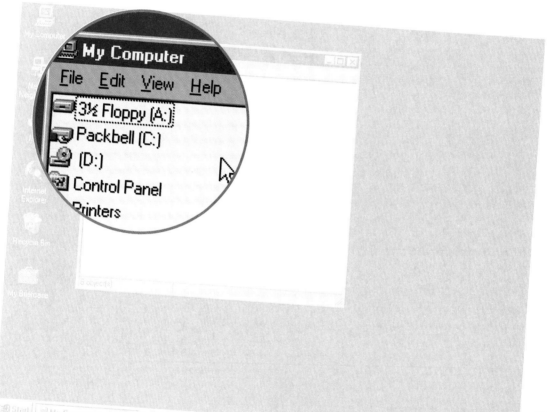

"Why would I do this?"

You will find that along with windows, menus are an invaluable way to work within Windows NT. Menus contain commands that allow you to perform the majority of your tasks. Most windows contain *menu bars* across the top of the window that list the available menus. At the end of this task is a table that contains information about what certain symbols mean on a menu.

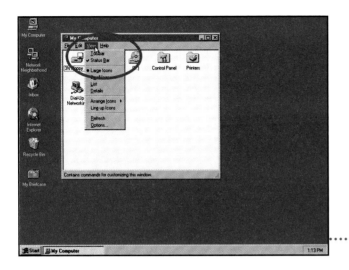

1 Open the window by double-clicking the **My Computer** icon. Notice the list of menus across the top of the window, just below the title bar. You should see File, Edit, View, and Help. Point over the word **View** with the mouse pointer and click the left mouse button. The View menu will open.

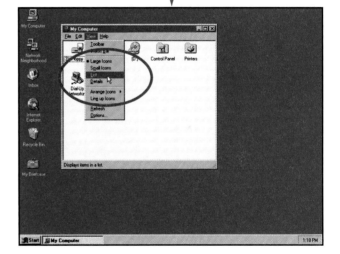

2 Click **List** to choose the command and close the menu. The icons in the My Computer window change to the name of the icon. To change them back, open the **View** menu again, and choose the **Large Icons** command. ■

Task 10: Using Menus

Reading Symbols on a Menu

Symbol	Description
Command with a Letter	Press the shortcut keys Underlined instead of accessing the menu the next time you want to perform that command. For example: **Alt+V** brings you to the **View** menu; then press **L** to select the **List** command.
Check Mark	This means the command is active. For example: The check beside the **View**, **Status Bar** command means the status bar is showing in the window. Notice at the bottom of the My Computer window where it says **6 object(s)**. Click the Status Bar command to remove the check mark. Now the My Computer window does not have a status bar at the bottom of the window. To add it back, select the **Status Bar** command from the **View** menu.
Bullet to the Left of a Command	If a bullet appears beside the command, this shows a command has been selected. Only one command in a menu may be selected at a time. For example, when you selected to view the My Computer window with a List instead of with Large Icons, the bullet moved from the left of Large Icons to the left of List. Try this again to see.
Arrow to the Right of a Command	This means that there are more options available to this command. For example, when you select the command **Arrange Icons** from the **View** menu of the My Documents window, a cascading menu will appear with choices. Try this and select **Auto Arrange**. This will arrange your icons in the My Computer window automatically. If you go back into this menu, you will see there is now a check mark to the left of the **Auto Arrange** command. You can select that command again to disable it if you like.
Ellipsis After a Command	This means a dialog box containing more information will appear if you select that command. For example, see Task 11, "Using a Dialog Box."
"Grayed Out" Commands	On a menu, any command that is not as bold or prominent as other commands. This means that the command is not available at that time. It cannot be selected. For example, if you want to Cut or Copy text, but have not highlighted any text, the Cut and Copy commands from the Edit menu, or shortcut menu, will be "grayed out," or not selectable.

Using a Dialog Box

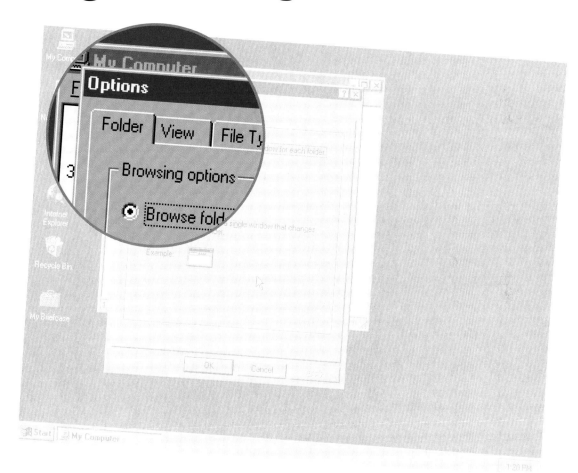

"Why would I do this?"

Dialog boxes contain options from which you can choose to control windows, applications, document formatting, and a host of other procedures. Dialog boxes are widespread in Windows; luckily, all dialog boxes have common elements and all are treated in a similar way. This task shows you how to open and maneuver a dialog box.

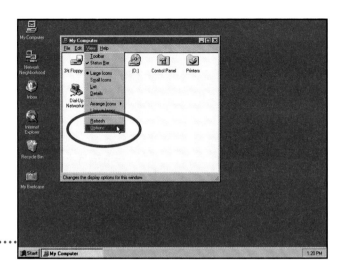

1 The **My Computer** window should be open. If it is not, double-click the **My Computer** icon. From the **View** menu, choose **Options**.

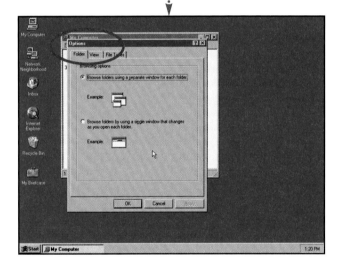

2 The Options dialog box appears. This particular dialog box contains three tabs which hold information and options relating to viewing windows as well as some features common to all dialog boxes. To view a tab's contents, click the tab. The following table describes options available in most dialog boxes. ■

Puzzled?

When a dialog box is open, most of the time you cannot perform any other actions on the desktop until you either accept changes by choosing **OK** or cancel the dialog box by choosing **Cancel**. A shortcut for accepting changes in a dialog box is to press the **Enter** key on the keyboard. Likewise, a shortcut to canceling the box (or any changes you do not want to keep) is to press the **Esc** key on the keyboard.

Parts of the Dialog Box

Element	Description
Tabs	These are pages within the dialog box that include specific options and information related to the dialog box. To view a tab, click it.
Radio buttons	These are round white buttons that contain a black bullet when selected. They are sometimes called option buttons. Choose an option to activate it. You can only choose one option in a group of options; choosing a second option deselects the first. For example, the View, Options dialog box set to the **Folder** tab is a radio button.
Check boxes	These are square boxes that indicate options. Select the options by clicking them; a check mark appears in the square box. You can check one or more check box options in a group.
List boxes	These are lists of available items (such as files) that you can scroll through and select from. Select an item by clicking it. The View, Options dialog box set to the **View** tab, option button **Hide files of these types** is an example of a list box.
Text boxes	These are boxes in which you can enter a measurement such as point sizes for fonts. An example would be the View, Options dialog box set to the **File Types** tab; select the **New Type** button and fill in the appropriate text. Make sure you cancel out of these dialog boxes if you are just trying the example. If you select the button **Apply** before you select **Cancel**, the changes will be saved.
Command buttons	Common command buttons include OK and Cancel. Click **OK** to accept the changes you made in a dialog box, or click **Cancel** to cancel all changes and close the dialog box. Other command buttons may lead you to another dialog box, and many perform an action.

12

Changing the Window Display

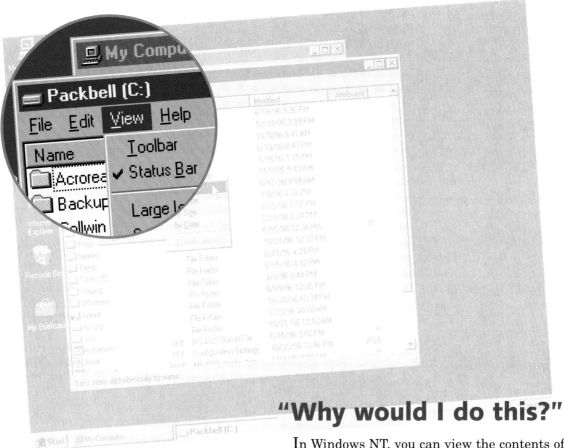

"Why would I do this?"

In Windows NT, you can view the contents of a window in a variety of ways. We have already talked about how to scroll and change a window view from icons to names. Wouldn't it be nice to view the contents of your windows alphabetically by name, or by the date they were last edited? It can make files, folders, and applications easier to find.

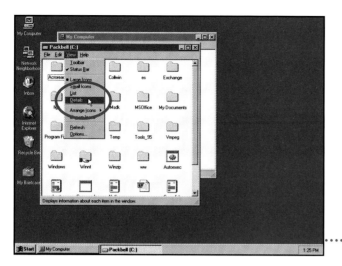

1 In the **My Computer** window, open your hard drive by double-clicking the icon that shares the name you gave, or that your computer was given. The icon name will also list the drive letter—usually (C:). Open the **View** menu and click the **Details** command. The window now displays elements in the list form. You may need to enlarge the window to view all the fine details.

2 Open the **View** menu and choose **Arrange Icons**. A secondary menu appears; choose **by Name**. The folders and files in the window are rearranged alphabetically, starting with folders first and then files. Notice that if you click the **Name** heading button just below the Menu, it will alternate the folder and file order from ascending to descending.

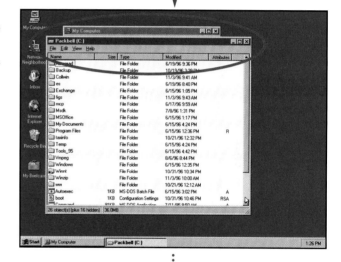

3 To change back to the original view, open the **View** menu and click the **List** command. You can resize the window if necessary. ■

Missing Link

Rearrange the icons in the window by dragging each one to a new location. If the icons will not move, open the **View** menu and click the **Arrange Icons** command. From the secondary menu, choose **Auto Arrange** so the check mark disappears.

Arranging Windows on the Desktop

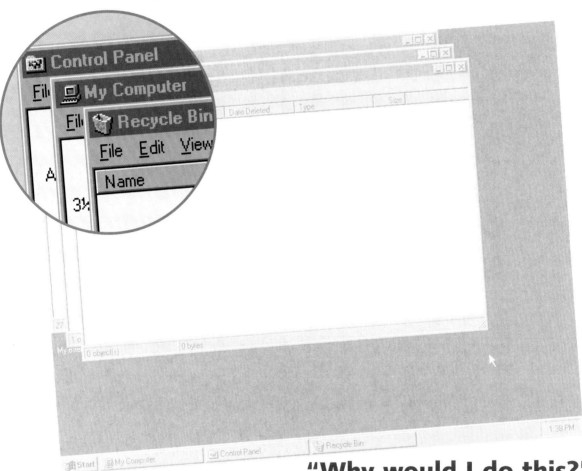

"Why would I do this?"

When you start working with multiple windows you will notice that they have a tendency to overlap one another. This can sometimes make it difficult to find what you want. Windows NT allows you to arrange the windows on the desktop in several different ways to make your work easier and more efficient.

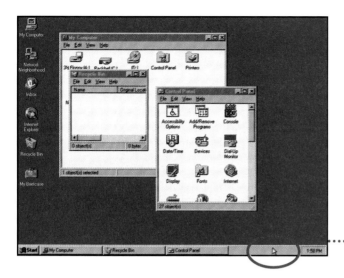

1 Open multiple windows on the desktop. I suggest the **My Computer**, **Control Panel**, and **My Briefcase** windows. Point to an area on the taskbar that is not covered with a button, or choose the system tray (containing the time). The taskbar shortcut menu will open.

2 From the shortcut menu, choose **Cascade** to display the windows in an orderly fashion. Windows NT arranges the open windows to overlap, and then resizes them so they are all the same size. To work in any window, click the mouse in the window to make it active. An active window moves to the front of the rest, and its title bar is a different color.

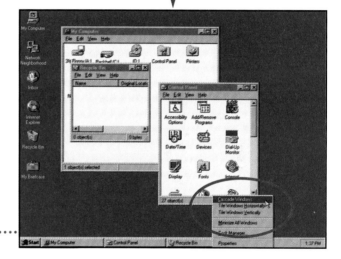

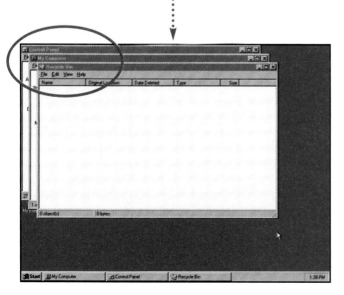

3 Click the right mouse button on the task bar and choose **Tile Horizontally** or **Tile Vertically** to rearrange the open windows in a different way. ■

Missing Link

If you do not care to have your windows cascaded or tiled, you can always resize the windows yourself. If you want all the windows minimized, you can select the **Minimize All Windows** command from the taskbar shortcut menu.

PART III

Working with Folders and Files

ONE OF THE MAIN GOALS of Windows NT is to have the complicated system information in the background so that you, the end user, do not have to worry about how your computer works. You can spend your time working. When you open up your *My Computer* window, it is set up so that everything appears to be an icon. These icons are of folders, files, and the drives available on your computer.

The *hard drive* on your computer is much like a filing cabinet. A filing cabinet has folders, files, and drawers. A hard drive has folders, files, and access to other drives (drawers). Your hard drive will have a letter associated with it to represent that drive. This letter is usually *C:* but can really be any letter. Also note that your other drives, like the floppy or CD-ROM drive, have letters associated with them too. These can all be viewed in the My Computer window or in the *Windows NT Explorer*.

Folder icons are used to represent each folder, which can in turn hold files and more folders and more files and more... You can open and close folders to view their contents, or you can create new folders to keep your saved information organized. In addition to creating new folders, you can copy or move an old folder to a new location. Sometimes it will be more appropriate to simply rename a folder instead of creating a new one.

As you save more information on your computer, it is a good idea to back up some of your folders and files to a floppy drive or another hard drive. When you do this, you can then delete the files from your computer. This is where the *Recycle Bin* comes in. The Recycle Bin is a folder that keeps the folders and files you have deleted until you tell the Recycle Bin to remove the files from your hard drive. In case you change your mind and do not wish to delete a folder or file, you can choose to restore the items from the Recycle Bin.

Once you have become accustomed to manipulating folders and files, you will need to keep track of your information. In case you forget where you have stored a folder or file, you can use the *Windows NT Find* feature to locate it. You can search by name, date, or other types of search criteria. If all you can remember is a portion of a file name, you can do a *wild card* search. This is where Windows NT finds any folder and file that has the portion of what you remember in the name. You can also search for file extensions like *.doc* files tend to be *MS Word* files, or *.xls* files tend to be *MS Excel* files.

All the Tasks in this Part can be done using *Shortcut Menus*. Shortcut menus are menus that appear when you have the mouse pointer over a particular item and click the right mouse button. These shortcut menus will allow you to manage folders and files, in a shorter amount of time, just like the name.

Another way to manage folders and files is by using the Windows NT Explorer. This program lets you open, create, copy, move, rename, delete, find, and manage folders and files all in one window. If you have used Windows 3.x or Windows 95, you will find the Windows NT Explorer to be similar to the File Manager and the Windows Explorer.

Opening Folders

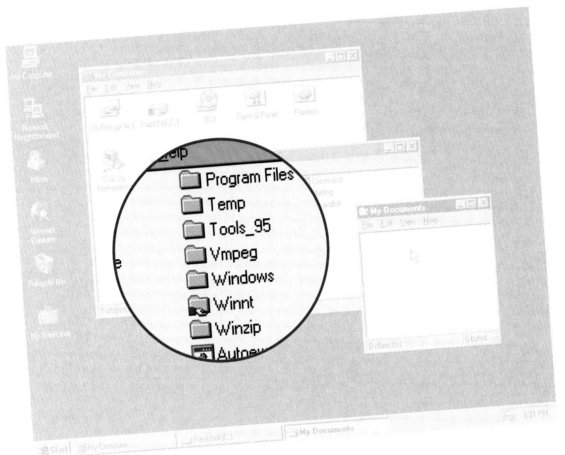

"Why would I do this?"

Folders contain files, programs, or other features you can use to do work in Windows NT. When you open a folder, you reveal the folder's contents in a window.

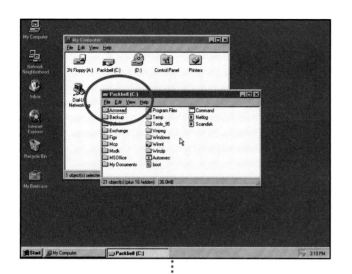

1 Double-click the **My Computer** icon on the desktop. The My Computer window opens. In the My Computer window, double-click the icon representing your hard drive. The drive window appears with icons representing folders and files on your hard drive.

Missing Link

An alternative to double-clicking the icon is to click once on the icon you wish to open, then open the File menu and choose the Open command.

2 Select the **My Documents** folder in the drive window by double-clicking the icon. If you do not have a My Documents folder, double-click any of the folders in the window. Practice this, then close the folders you have opened by clicking on the (x) in the upper right corner of the title bar. ■

Puzzled?

Your **My Documents** folder might contain many folders and files, or it might not have any. Either way is okay.

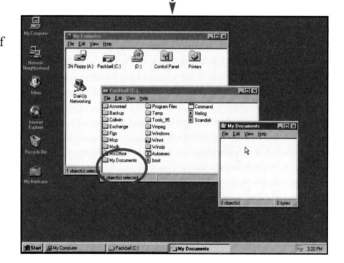

45

TASK

15

Creating Folders

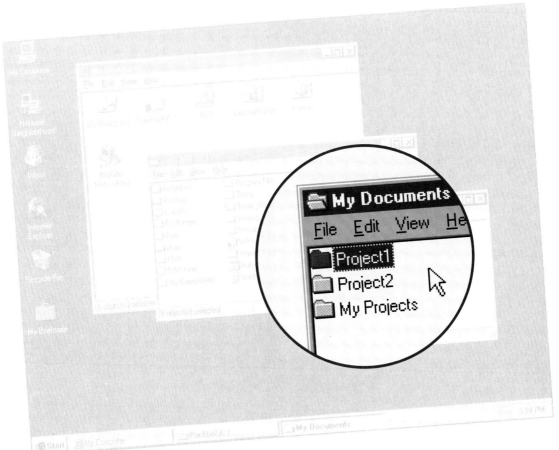

"Why would I do this?"

Once you start working with a lot of files, you will find it easier to group them together in folders. Some people group their folders by project, person, or topic; you can group files and other folders any way you want.

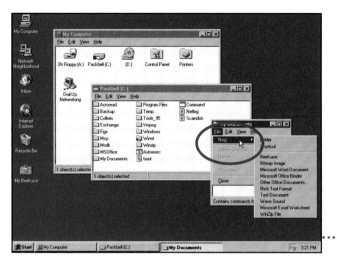

1 Open the **My Documents** window (or whatever window you choose to open instead). From the **File** menu of the **My Documents** window, choose the **New** command. A secondary menu appears.

2 From the secondary menu, choose the **Folder** command. The new folder appears in the drive window.

Missing Link

Another way to create a new folder is to right click once in a window. From the Shortcut Menu, select the New command; then from the secondary menu, select Folder.

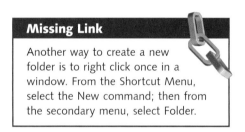

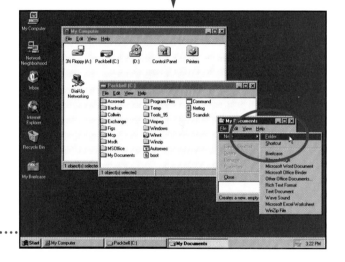

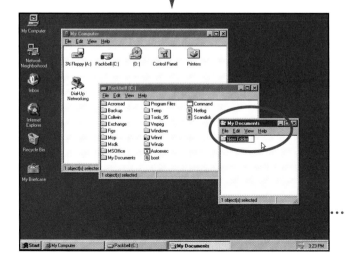

3 Notice that the new folder is titled **"New Folder"** and has a rectangular box around it with the name highlighted. This rectangular box signifies that you can edit the name. Enter a new name for the folder (I chose **Project1**); when you type, the old name disappears. Press **Enter** when you finish typing to accept the new name.

4 Now the new folder **Project1** is displayed in the **My Documents** window. Try creating two more folders inside the **My Documents** folder. Title the two other folders **Project2** and **My Projects**. ■

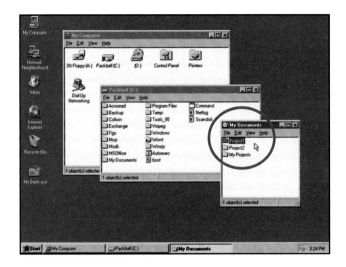

Copying Folders and Files

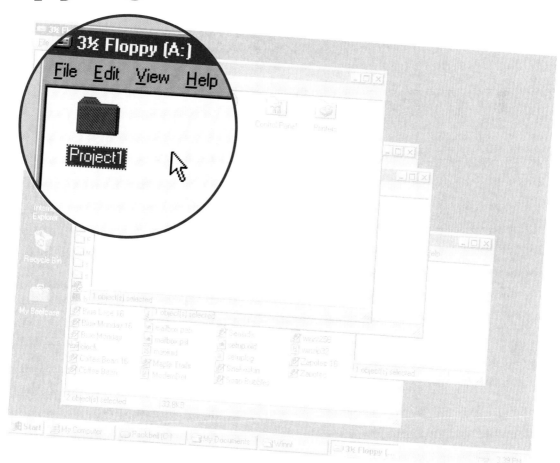

"Why would I do this?"

You will find that many times when you are
working with folders and files, you will want to
make a copy of your work. You might want to
create a backup of your work onto a disk, or for
the purpose of working on another computer.
Instead of creating a new folder and copying all
of the files into it, you can simply copy the folder, and all the files it contains will be copied as
well.

Task 16: Copying Folders and Files

1 From the drive window, open the **Winnt** folder. Select the file titled **Seaside** by clicking on it once. While holding down the Control key, click once also on the file **Solstice**.

Puzzled?

If you do not have a **Winnt** folder, your Windows NT folder is probably **Windows**. In addition, if you do not have the Seaside or Solstice files, practice this Part with any other two files you choose.

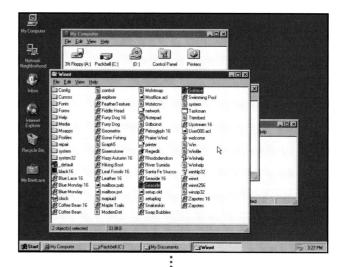

2 Open the **Edit** menu and choose the **Copy** command to copy the file.

3 The **My Documents** window should still be open on your desktop, make it the active window. Double-click the new folder you created in the last task (**Project1**).

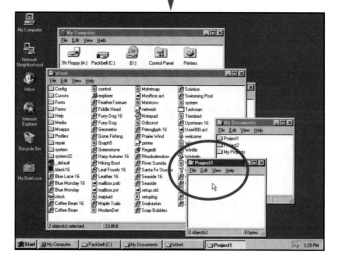

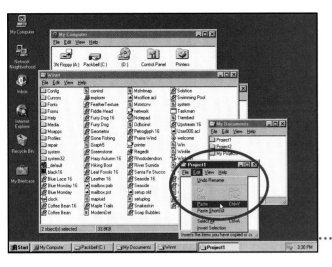

4 Open the **Edit** menu and choose the **Paste** command to copy the file. The files **Seaside** and **Solstice** will now appear in the **Project1** window.

5 Close the **Project1** window and click once on **Project1**. From the **Edit** menu of the **My documents** window, select the **Copy** command. This will copy the **Project1** folder and the files **Seaside** and **Solstice** contained inside.

Missing Link

When copying files to a floppy drive, you can drag and drop the file to the floppy drive window instead of Copy and Paste. Copying the file automatically is the default when using floppy drives.

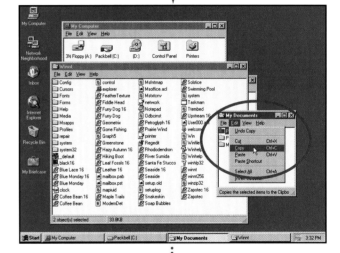

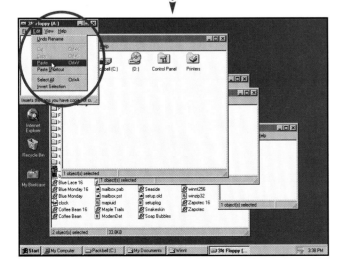

6 Insert a disk in your floppy disk drive. From the **My Computer** window, double-click the drive icon for your floppy disk. In the floppy drive window, open the **Edit** menu and choose **Paste**. Windows copies the new folder, and its contents (Seaside and Solstice). A message box will show that the files are being copied. Once the files are copied over, close the **Drive A** window. ■

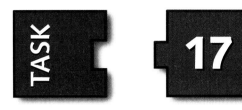

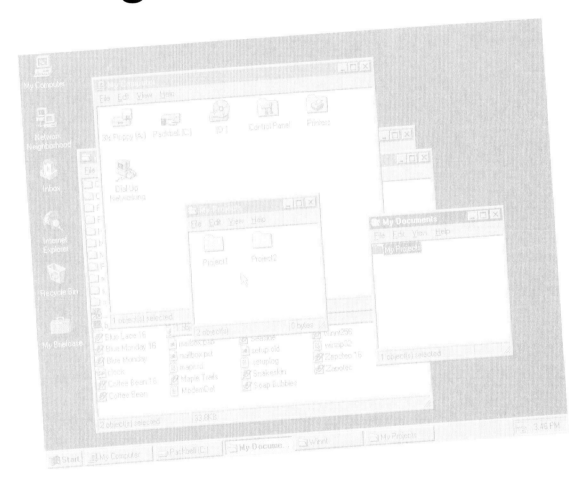

Moving Folders and Files

"Why would I do this?"

You can move a folder and its contents to another folder or to a disk so you can reorganize your saved files and folders. If you have numerous files related to one particular subject, you might create a folder and move all the appropriate files to that folder.

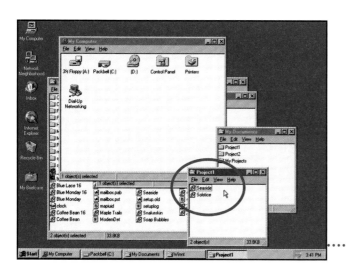

1 From the **My Documents** window, select and open the **Project1** folder.

2 Click once on the **Seaside** file, so that it is highlighted. Open the **Edit** menu and choose the **Cut** command to move the folder. The menu closes and only a ghost of the cut folder shows in the window. This action moves the folder to the Clipboard until you're ready to paste it.

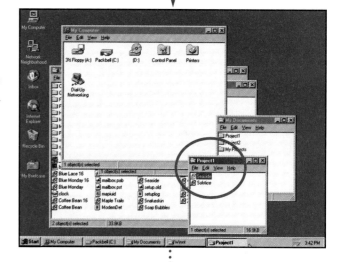

Puzzled?

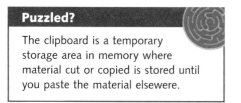

The clipboard is a temporary storage area in memory where material cut or copied is stored until you paste the material elsewere.

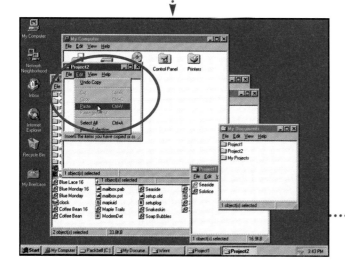

3 Double-click the **Project2** folder in the **My Documents** window. In the **Project2** window, open the **Edit** menu and choose **Paste**. Windows moves the file to the new folder.

4 Close the Project1 and Project2 windows. In the My Documents window, select the **Project1** and **Project2** folders with the Control key. Now click once on top of the two folders and hold the mouse button down. Drag the two folders on top of the **My Projects** folder. When the My Projects folder becomes highlighted, release the mouse button. This will automatically move the two folders and all their contents into the My projects folder.

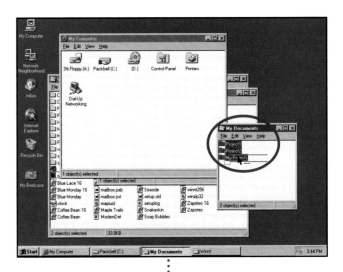

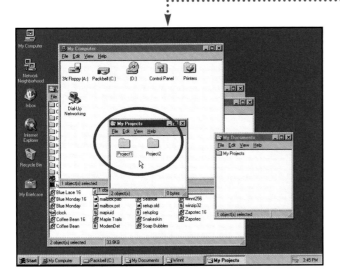

5 Open the **My Projects** folder and you will see that the folders and files have been moved. ■

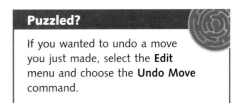

Puzzled?

If you wanted to undo a move you just made, select the **Edit** menu and choose the **Undo Move** command.

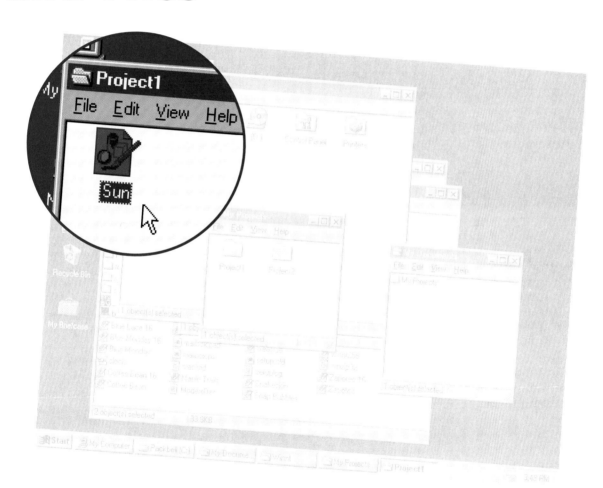

Renaming Folders and Files

"Why would I do this?"

As you add more folders and files to your computer, you will find the need to rearrange and reorganize folders and files. Windows NT lets you easily rename folders to help you better organize your computer work.

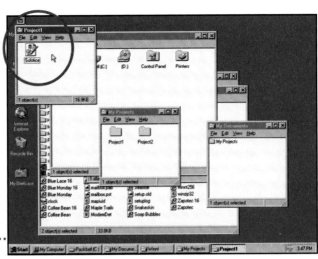

1 Click the **My Documents** title bar so that it is the active window. Open up the **My Projects** folder and the **Project1** folder.

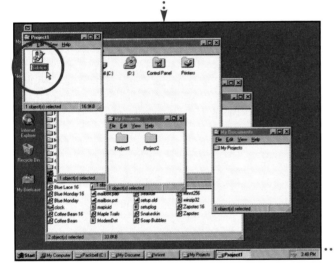

2 Click the file **Solstice** once to highlight it. Click again directly on the file name and a rectangular box with the name highlighted will appear. The blinking cursor will be displayed at the end of the word **Solstice**.

3 Enter the new name for the file, **Sun,** and press **Enter** to accept the name.

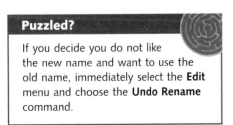

Puzzled?

If you decide you do not like the new name and want to use the old name, immediately select the **Edit** menu and choose the **Undo Rename** command.

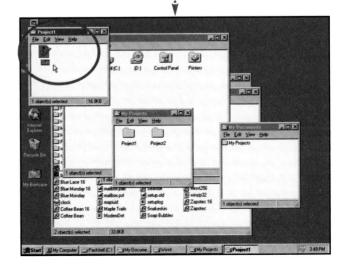

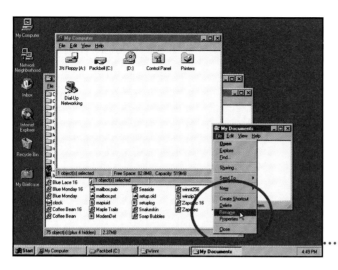

4 Now close the **Project1** and **My Projects** folders. Highlight the **My Projects** folder in the My Documents window (it will probably already be highlighted). Open the **File** menu and choose the **Rename** command.

5 Enter the new name for the folder (**Projects 1-7**) and press **Enter** to accept the name. ■

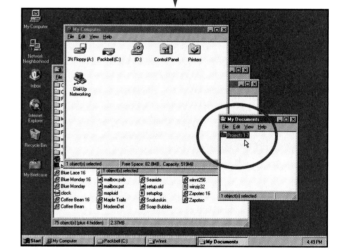

Missing Link

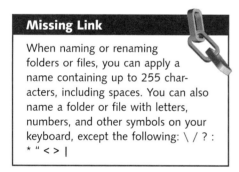

When naming or renaming folders or files, you can apply a name containing up to 255 characters, including spaces. You can also name a folder or file with letters, numbers, and other symbols on your keyboard, except the following: \ / ? : * " < > |

Deleting Folders and Files

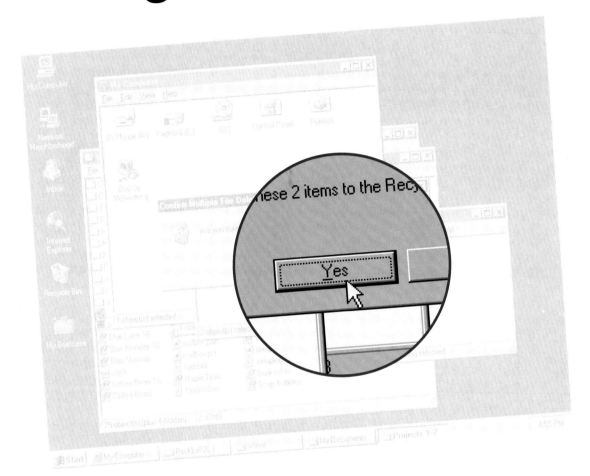

"Why would I do this?"

You delete folders and files when you no longer need them or when you have copied them elsewhere as a backup and do not need two copies. When you delete a folder, remember you also delete its contents, including other folders and their contents. Windows NT moves deleted folders to the *Recycle Bin*.

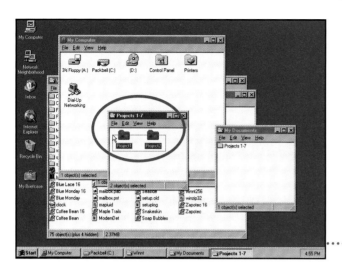

1 Open the **Projects 1-7** folder. Select the folder or folders you want to delete. Lets use **Project1** and **Project2** as examples. Select them both using the mouse. Click and drag the pointer to highlight both folders.

2 Open the **File** menu and choose the **Delete** command.

Missing Link

If you change your mind about deleting the folders, choose the **No** button in the **Confirm Folder Delete** message box. In addition, you can always open the **Edit** menu and choose the **Undo Delete** command.

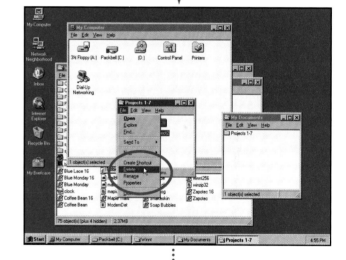

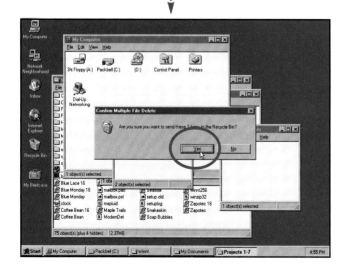

3 A **Confirm Folder Delete** message box appears and asks you if you are sure you want to remove the folders and move the contents to the **Recycle Bin**. Choose **Yes** to delete the selected folders; the confirmation box closes and the folders disappear. ■

Using the Recycle Bin

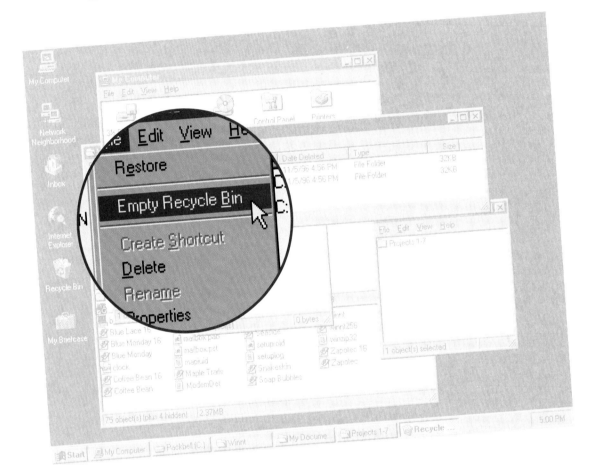

"Why would I do this?"

The Recycle Bin is where you put folders and files that you want deleted or are considering deleting. These folders and files will be moved to your Recycle Bin. The Recycle Bin will allow you to remove the folders and files from your hard drive, or restore them to the location you deleted them from.

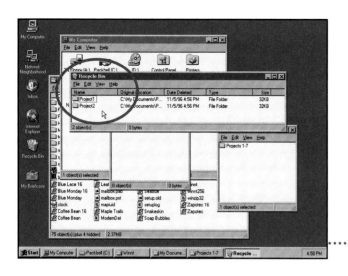

1 Open the **Recycle Bin** icon on the desktop. The **Recycle Bin** will contain the folders **Project1** and **Project2** and detailed information about the file name, original location, date deleted, type, and size. You might need to resize the Recycle Bin window.

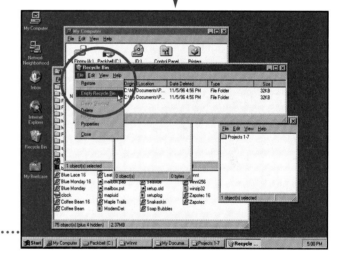

2 Select the folder **Project2**. From the **File** menu choose the **Empty Recycle Bin** command.

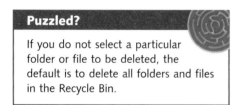

Puzzled?

If you do not select a particular folder or file to be deleted, the default is to delete all folders and files in the Recycle Bin.

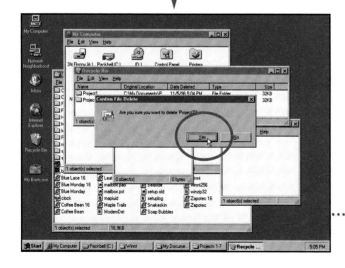

3 A message box will appear and ask you if you are sure you want to delete the Project2 folder. If you choose **Yes**, the file will be deleted from your hard drive. If you choose **No**, you can always come back to the items in the Recycle Bin later. Choose **Yes**.

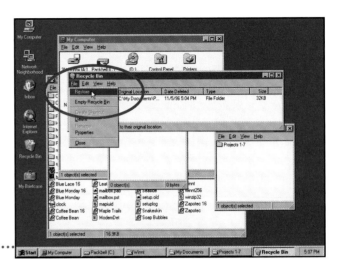

4 Instead of deleting folders or files in the Recycle Bin, you might want to restore them. Select the folder **Project1**. From the **File** menu choose **Restore**.

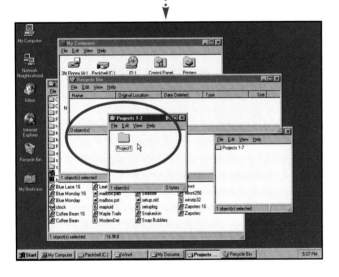

5 The **Project1** folder will be returned to the **Projects 1-7** folder. ■

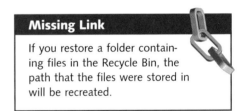

Missing Link

If you restore a folder containing files in the Recycle Bin, the path that the files were stored in will be recreated.

Finding Folders and Files

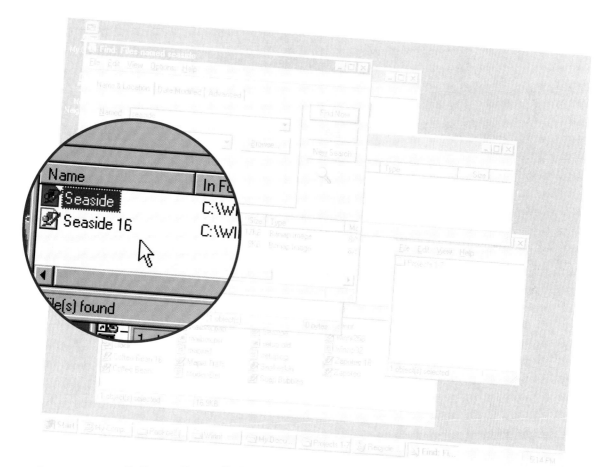

"Why would I do this?"

After working for months with your applications, your computer becomes filled with various folders and files, making it hard for you to remember where everything is. Windows NT includes a command that helps you locate specific files or folders by name, file type, location of the file, and so on.

Task 21: Finding Folders and Files

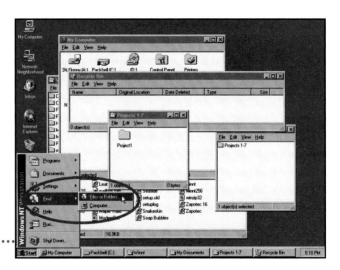

1 Open the **Start** menu and choose the **Find** command. A secondary menu appears. From the secondary menu, choose **Files or Folders**.

2 The **Find: All Files** dialog box appears. The default tab showing is **Name & Location**. In the named text box, enter the name of the file you want to search for.

Missing Link

You can use the characters * and ? (known as wild cards) in your search. For example, to find all files ending with the extension xls, you could type *.xls. You could type doc??.* to find all the files beginning with doc followed by two characters and ending in any extension.

3 To change the drive of the search, click the down arrow next to the drop down list box and choose the floppy or CD-ROM drive from the drop-down list. Remember, there has to be a disk in the floppy or CD-ROM drive first, or you will get an error.

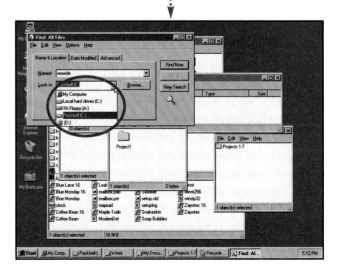

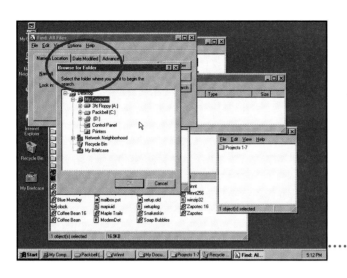

4 You can choose **Browse** and then double-click a specific folder in the **Browse for Folder** dialog box. For now, choose the **Cancel** button to close the Browse for Folder dialog box.

5 Click the **Find Now** button to initiate the search for the file name. Windows NT displays a list of files at the bottom of the dialog box. You might need to enlarge the dialog box to see all the file information.

Missing Link

Once you have found the folder or file you are looking for, double-click it, and Windows NT will open the folder or file and its associated application.

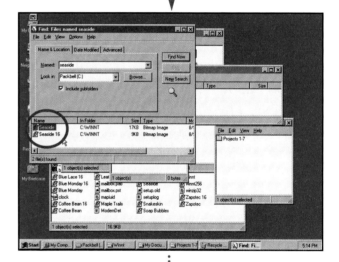

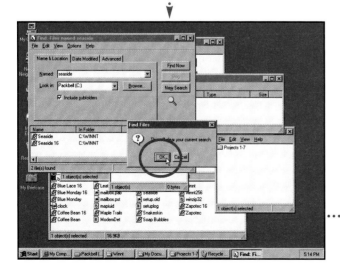

Missing Link

At any time you can select the **Stop** button to halt the search.

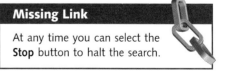

6 Click the **New Search** button to search for a new folder or file. A warning message appears stating that the previous search will be cleared. Choose **OK**.

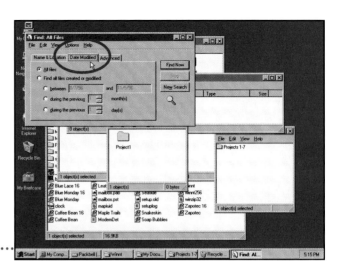

7 If you were working on a file yesterday, but you cannot remember what you named it. From the **Find: All Files** dialog box, select the **Date Modified** tab.

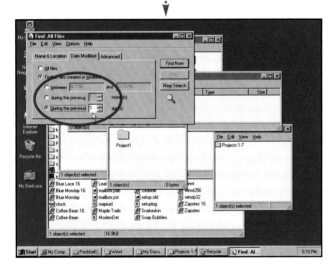

8 Select the **during the previous** radio button and scroll the arrows on the right of the text box to the appropriate number of days. Since it was yesterday, select **1** (it will go to the entire 24 hours of yesterday, not just the previous 24 hours). Choose the **Find Now** button and you can search through the files to find the one you are looking for. When you are finished, close out of the Find: All Files dialog box. ■

Puzzled?

There is also an **Advanced** tab on the Find: All Files dialog box. This is for advanced searches. You could search your hard disk folder C:\My Documents for a file named work??.* that was created within the past 5 days, that contains the string "marketing proposal" in the document.

Managing Folders and Files with Shortcut Menus

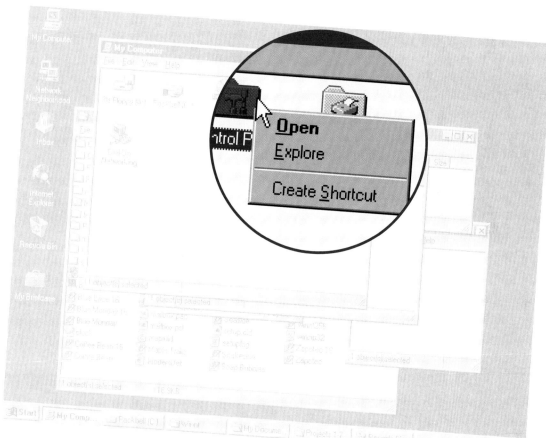

"Why would I do this?"

Use the shortcut menu to cut, copy, or paste folders and files to another location. It is also handy to rename or delete folders and files with the shortcut menu. You will find that managing folders and files using the shortcut menu makes your work faster and easier.

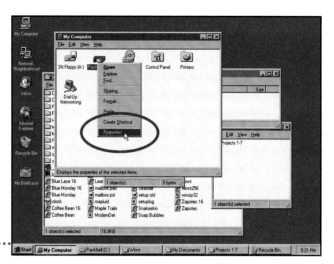

1 Click the **My Computer** window title bar to make it the active window. Click the hard drive icon once. To display a shortcut menu, point the mouse at the folder or file and click the right mouse button. The shortcut menu appears. Choose the **Properties** command.

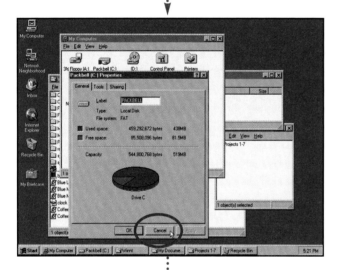

2 A **Properties** dialog box appears. The **General** tab that is displayed shows how much hard drive space you have used on your computer. Close this dialog box by selecting the **Cancel** button.

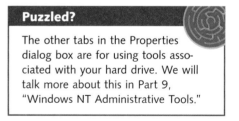

Puzzled?

The other tabs in the Properties dialog box are for using tools associated with your hard drive. We will talk more about this in Part 9, "Windows NT Administrative Tools."

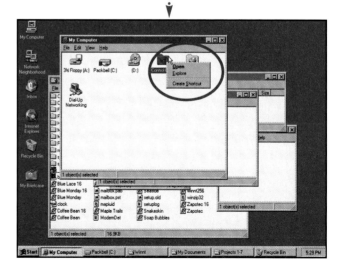

3 Try clicking on the **Control Panel** or other folders and files to see the different shortcut menus. ■

Using the Windows NT Explorer

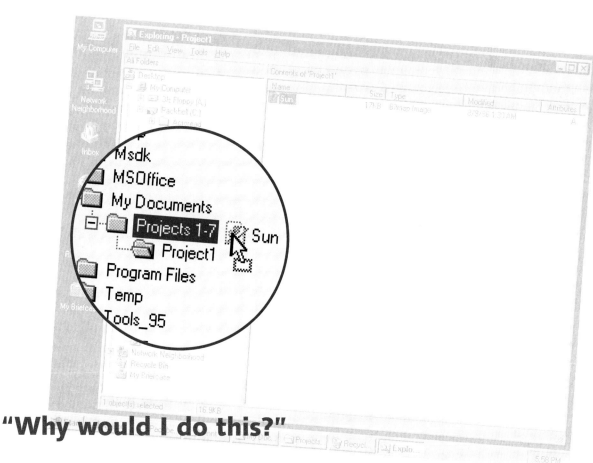

"Why would I do this?"

So far in Part 3, you have learned how to manipulate folders and files so you can work more efficiently. Now that you can manage your folders and files, this is where the Windows NT Explorer comes in. The Windows NT Explorer is the fastest, easiest way to copy, move, create, rename and view folders. Whether you use the Windows NT Explorer window or not, you will see how useful it can be.

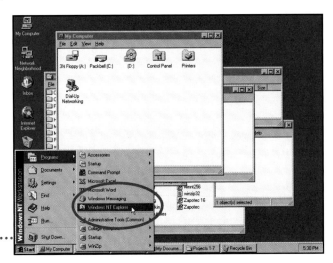

1 To open the Windows NT Explorer, click the **Start** button and choose **Programs** from the menu. This will list the programs that you have installed on your computer. Choose the **Windows NT Explorer**.

2 The Windows NT Explorer window appears. Notice that the Explorer window has two distinct groupings. The left side of the split Explorer window lists all drives and folders on the hard drive. Any folder with a plus sign (+) in front of it represents a folder containing more folders and files. Click the plus sign and any additional folders within that main folder, will display. Click the folder and the folder's contents appear on the right side of the Explorer window. Double-click the folder and any folders it contains also appear under it on the left side of the window.

3 Double-click any folder on the right side of the Explorer window to display the contents of that folder. If you should double-click a file, such as a document file or program file, you would open that file and/or application. When you display folder contents on the right side of the Explorer window, the details are shown by default. You can change the display to large icons, small icons, a list, or details.

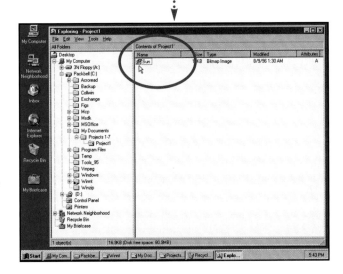

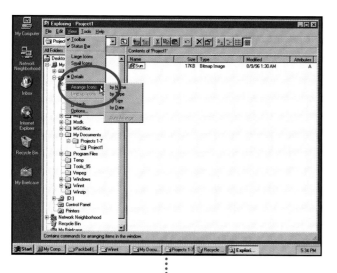

4 Choose **View**, **Arrange Icons** to sort the files by type, date, size, or name, just as you would in the My Computer window.

Missing Link

You also can choose View and show the files as large or small icons and display or hide the Toolbar and status bar of the Explorer window. Additionally, you can choose the Edit menu and cut, copy, and paste any folder or file, just as you would in the My Computer window.

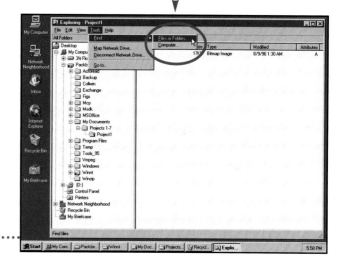

5 Choose **Tools, Find** and select **Files or Folders**. The **Find: All Files** dialog box will appear. You can search for any folder or file, just as described in Task 21.

6 With the Windows NT Explorer, you can copy files by the drag and drop method. Drag a file from the right side of the Explorer window to the left side, and drop it on top of the folder to which you want it copied. If you see a black circle with a line through it, that means you cannot drop the file at that location. When you release the mouse button, the file is dropped, or copied, to the last location of the mouse.

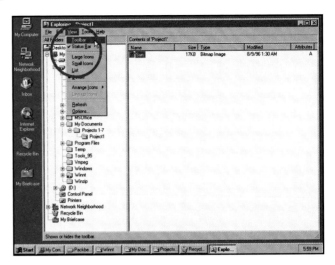

Task 23: Using the Windows NT Explorer

7 Select the **View** menu and choose the **Toolbar** command. This will display a toolbar that will allow you to click buttons associated with menu commands. You can utilize the toolbar on any window you open that has a View, Toolbar command. ■

Window Toolbar Buttons

Click this	Action
Project1	The Go to a different folder is a drop down list box of drives and directories. When the left side of the split Explorer window is so long that you have to scroll down to get to a particular location, thus you cannot see where you were at previous. This feature will allow you to jump location quickly.
⬆	The Up One Level button takes you up one directory level from anywhere on the Explorer window.
🖥	The Map Network Drive button connects you to shared directories on the network and assigns (maps) a drive letter to a shared network resource.
🖥	The Disconnect Network Drive button allows you to remove a drive-letter assignment and disconnects you from shared directories.
✂	The Cut button will copy and remove a folder or file and store that item on the Clipboard.
📋	The Copy button will copy a folder or file and store that item on the Clipboard.
📋	The Paste button will take an item from the Clipboard and insert it where you choose.
↺	The Undo button will cancel an action within a program.
✕	The Delete button will remove a folder or file and place it in the Recycle Bin for removal from the hard drive or restoration.
🖼	The Properties button will call up the properties associated with that particular folder or file.
⬚	The Large Icons button will display the folders and files in the large icon view.

Click this	Action
	The Small Icons button will display the folders and files in the small icon view.
	The List button will display the folders and files in a list view.

PART IV

Controlling Applications

NUMEROUS COMPANIES PRODUCE software applications to work with a computer's operating system. Companies create word processing, database, spreadsheet, drawing, programming, design, and other kinds of software. Windows NT is an operating system that requires the software companies to follow guidelines to become *Windows* certified. *Windows* certified means that the application will run under the Windows 95 and Windows NT operating systems. This allows Windows NT to control all your programs (also called applications) the same way.

The best way to install all certified applications, is through an Add/Remove Programs dialog box. This way, you can easily install or uninstall applications through the Wizards that are available to you. These Wizards walk you through procedures to make sure that software is installed or uninstalled properly. You will probably need to use either your floppy or CD-ROM drive in connection with an *executable* (.EXE extension) file. Common executable files are install.exe or setup.exe, and they initiate the installation process. Files that start and operate your new application are copied to your hard disk, in a location that Windows NT can manipulate.

One of the biggest advantages of using Windows NT is the control it gives you over your applications. Windows NT applications are easy to open and use. Using the Start menu, you can select the application from the Programs menu, and the application will open automatically. Additionally, you can start an application by double-clicking on the executable file, or even a saved file that was created by the application.

Windows NT also includes a method of starting an application when you start your Windows NT session. This can save you time, especially if there is a specific application or file you use every time you start Windows NT. When you are finished using an application, you will probably want to save your work. Whether you save your work or not, you can always close the application. Windows NT has three quick ways to properly exit out of a program.

If there is an application that you want quick access to, you can add a *shortcut* to your desktop or anywhere on your hard disk. A shortcut is a small file that *points* (directs Windows NT) to your application, bypassing the use of menus. As quickly as you can create a shortcut, you can delete one any time you want. By working with

shortcuts, instead of application executables, the risk of deleting programs improperly is reduced. Finally, one more way that Windows NT makes starting applications easier, is by allowing you to add items to the Start menu. You can add, move, or delete a *command* on the Start menu, or any of the secondary menus off the Start menu. These commands are a quick way for you to access files, folders, or applications in Windows NT.

Installing and Uninstalling Windows Applications

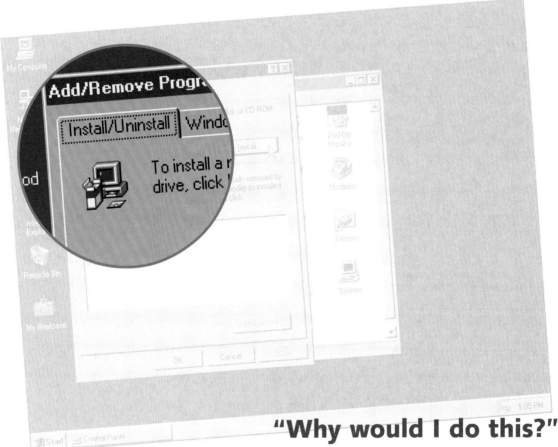

"Why would I do this?"

Windows NT comes with many useful applications. For example, a word processor, graphics program, and a Web browser are included. However, these applications may be too limited for certain tasks or incapable of them altogether. In this task, you will learn how to install any application that Windows NT will run and how to uninstall (remove) an application from Windows NT.

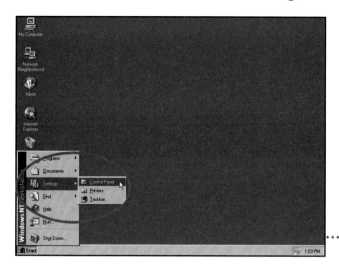

1 Insert your setup disk in either the floppy or CD-ROM drive. Open the **Start** menu and choose the **Settings** command. From the secondary menu, choose the **Control Panel**.

2 The **Control Panel** window will appear. Double-click the **Add/Remove Programs** icon.

Missing Link

Another way to install an application is by opening the **Start** menu and choosing the **Run** command. In the Open list box, type in the name of or browse for the startup/install file. Click **OK.** This will also take you to the Setup window, though, installing applications this way makes them difficult to delete using the Uninstall.

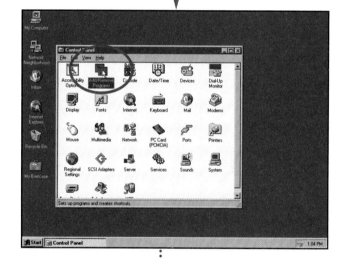

3 The **Add/Remove Programs Properties** dialog box will appear. In the **Install/Uninstall** tab, click the **Install** button.

Puzzled?

If you notice the application that you want to install is in the list box at the bottom of the Install/Uninstall tab, you can exit the install by clicking the **Cancel** button. This means the application is already installed on your computer or it was deleted from your computer without using the Uninstall program with Windows NT.

4 The **Install Program From Floppy Disk or CD-ROM** dialog box appears. Click the **Next** button. This will search your floppy and CD-ROM drives for install or setup files.

Missing Link

If the application you wish to remove does not show up in the Add/Remove list box, the application probably does not use the Windows NT system registry. This means you will need to see the specific software documentation to remove the program.

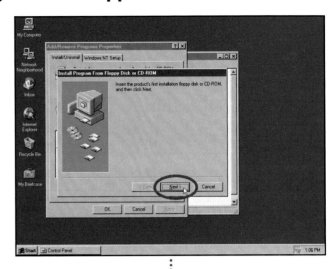

5 The **Run Installation Program** dialog box will display the file it found to install your application. Make sure that it found the file in the correct location. If it is not correct, click the **Browse** button and search for the file. Choose the **Finish** button and Windows NT installs the application. Make sure you keep an eye on the installation for any questions you may be asked. In addition, you may need to change disks, or follow on-screen instructions. When you have finished installing the application, choose **OK** from the **Add/Remove Programs Properties** dialog box. If you decide to stop the installation, choose the **Cancel** button.

6 If you want to remove an application from Windows NT, instead of choosing the Install button from the Add/Remove Programs Properties dialog box, select the Windows NT certified application listed in the **Add/Remove** list box. Then, choose the **Add/Remove** button. A message dialog box will appear asking you if you wish to continue removing the application you selected. If you want to continue, choose **Yes**; if not, choose **No** and cancel out of the **Add/Remove Programs Properties** dialog box by choosing the **Cancel** button. ■

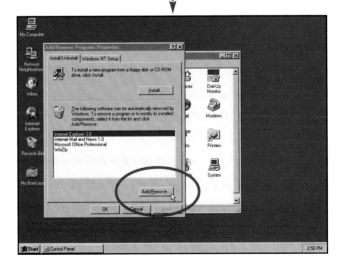

Starting an Application with the Start Menu

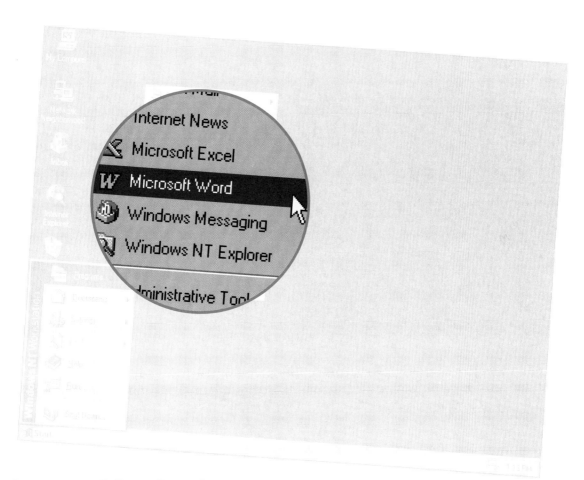

"Why would I do this?"

Windows NT Provides a hierarchical menu that gives you access to applications by group or type. This menu is accessed with the Start button. This can be one of the quickest and easiest ways to start an application in Windows NT.

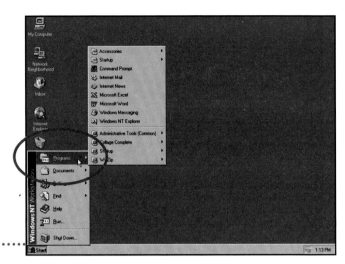

1 Open the **Start** menu and choose the **Programs** command. The **Programs** menu will appear. On the **Programs** menu, select the program group that contains the application you want to start. The folder's contents appear on a secondary menu.

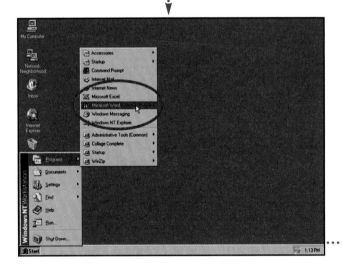

2 Click the application you want to start. I am going to choose **Microsoft Word**.

3 The Microsoft Word application opens in its own window. You can minimize the application window if you want. ■

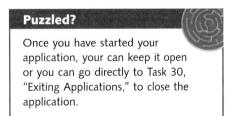

Puzzled?

Once you have started your application, your can keep it open or you can go directly to Task 30, "Exiting Applications," to close the application.

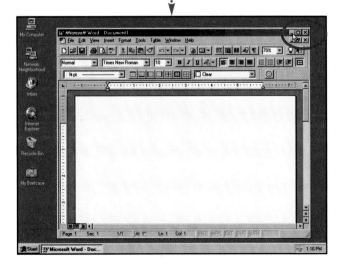

Starting an Application from a File

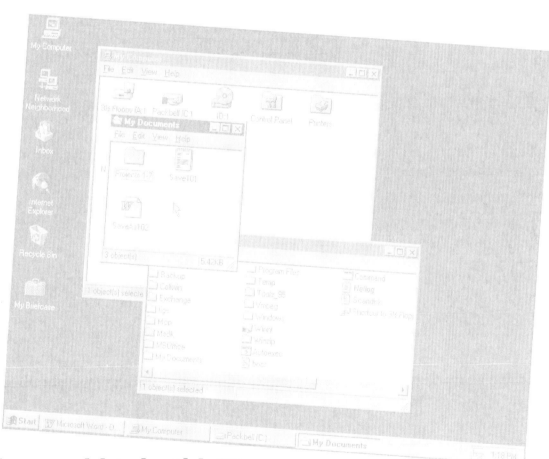

"Why would I do this?"

If the file you wish to work on is readily available (on your desktop, for example), it is quicker to access the application it was created in by double-clicking the file. This action eliminates two steps. First, you don't have to start the application; and second, you don't have to go through the process of opening the file within the application.

1 Open the **My Computer** window and double-click your hard drive window.

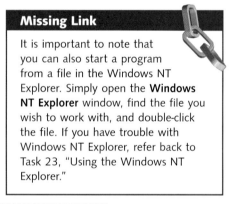

2 Open the **My Documents** folder to display all folders and files you have saved there. Double-click any file created in an application on your machine.

Missing Link

It is important to note that you can also start a program from a file in the Windows NT Explorer. Simply open the **Windows NT Explorer** window, find the file you wish to work with, and double-click the file. If you have trouble with Windows NT Explorer, refer back to Task 23, "Using the Windows NT Explorer."

3 The application opens with the file ready to work on. You can minimize this application window if you want. ■

Missing Link

You might double-click a file and get an error message. This is because Windows NT could not find the application associated with the file. For example, you double-click a file named flower.pdf and Windows NT gives you an error message; a list box appears to let you select the application to open the file.

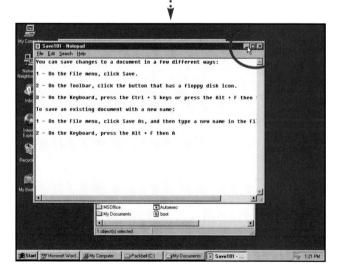

TASK 27

Starting an Application from Windows NT

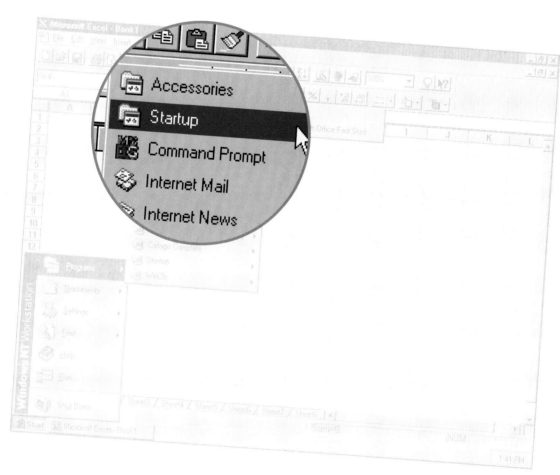

"Why would I do this?"

You may find that you use an application every time you use windows NT. Or, there may be a file that you will be working on for the next month. By placing an application or file in the Windows NT Startup folder, it will automatically start every time you start Windows NT.

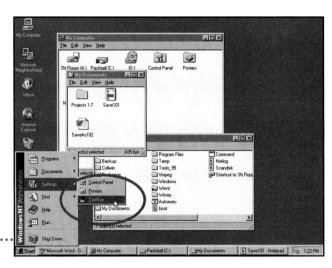

1 Open the **Start** menu and choose the **Settings** command. The Settings menu will appear. On the **Settings** menu, click **Taskbar**.

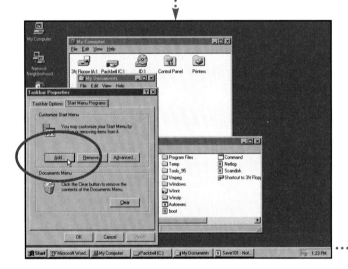

2 From the **Taskbar Properties** dialog box, choose the **Start Menu Programs** tab. Click the **Add** button.

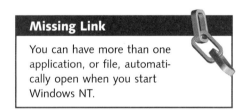

Missing Link

You can have more than one application, or file, automatically open when you start Windows NT.

3 The **Create Shortcut** dialog box will appear. Click the **Browse** button to open the **Browse** window.

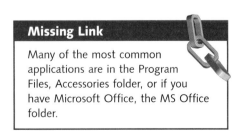

Missing Link

Many of the most common applications are in the Program Files, Accessories folder, or if you have Microsoft Office, the MS Office folder.

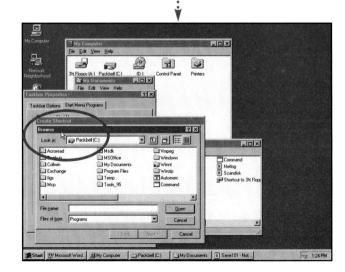

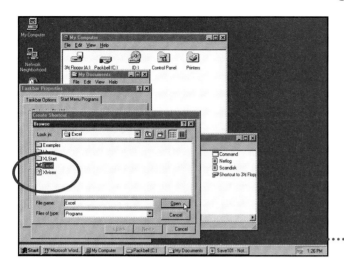

4 From the **Browse** window, locate the program you want to start with Windows NT. We are going to use the **Microsoft Excel** program for this Task. Use the **Look in** drop down list box like you use the Windows NT Explorer. When you have found the program, either double-click the program, or select it and click the **Open** button.

5 The **Create Shortcut** dialog box will appear again, but this time it will list the program you have selected. Click the **Next** button.

Missing Link

Notice that Programs is in the Files of type list box. This will help you locate programs specifically. You can, though, select **All files** from the drop down list box and start a file instead. The file you select will automatically start the application and open the file, when you start Windows NT.

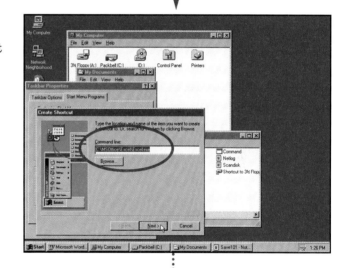

6 From the **Select Program Folder** dialog box, choose the **Startup** folder. Click the **Next** button.

Puzzled?

You can choose other folders aside from the Startup folder. This will be covered in Task 32, "Adding items to the Start Menu."

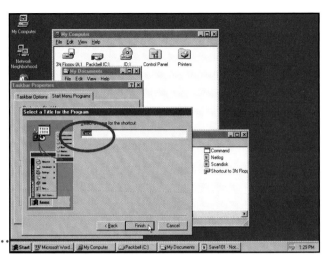

7 The **Select a Title for the Program** dialog box will appear and you can type in any name you wish. Click the **Finish** button. If Windows NT asks you to choose an icon, click one and then click **Finish**. Choose **OK** in the Taskbar Properties dialog box to close it and return to the desktop.

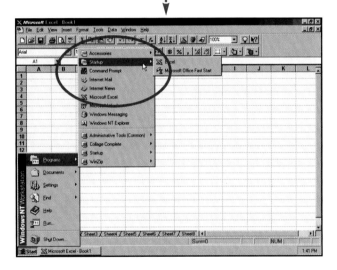

8 To test your startup link, either log out of Windows NT and log back in, or shut down the computer and start it back up (see Part I, "Getting Started with Windows NT"). The item(s) you selected to startup will start. Then, open the **Start** menu and choose the **Programs** command. You can see there is a Startup folder at the top and bottom of your Programs menu. The top Startup folder is your personal Windows NT profile. You can see that the Excel application is now in the Startup folder. The bottom Startup folder is for all user accounts on your computer. ■

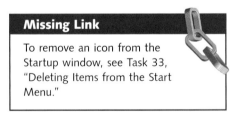

Missing Link

To remove an icon from the Startup window, see Task 33, "Deleting Items from the Start Menu."

Saving Your Work

"Why would I do this?"

Work created in applications must be saved to a file so that it can be accessed later. You can choose the name and location of the file for easy retrieval. This task will show you how to save a file in Word.

1 If you did not test step 8 in the last task to see your startup items, you should already have Microsoft Word open on your desktop (or minimized). If you do not, refer to Task 25, "Starting an Application with the Start Menu." Make Word the active window by clicking once on the title bar, or clicking once on the **Word** button on the taskbar.

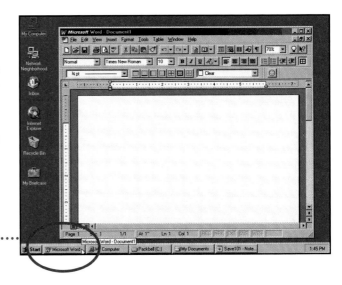

2 From the **File** menu, choose the **Save** command.

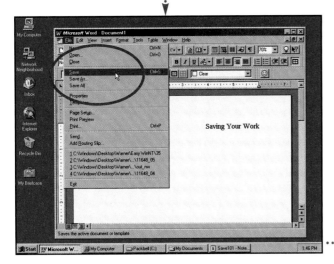

Missing Link

To save your work from the Keyboard, press the **Ctrl+S** keys or press the **Alt+F** then **S** keys.

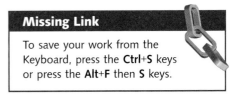

3 The **Save As** dialog box will appear. You can alter the where you save your documents, by clicking once on the **Save in** drop down list box and selecting your preferred folder. Choose the **My Documents** folder.

Missing Link

The **Save As** dialog box will only appear the first time you save the document. This is so you can give it a name and save it to your desired location. Afterwards, choosing **File**, **Save** will save the document to the current name and location.

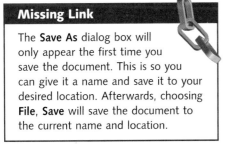

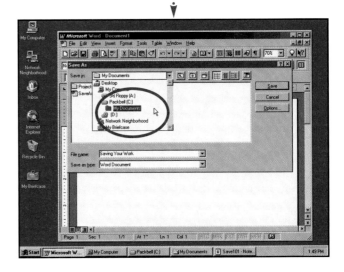

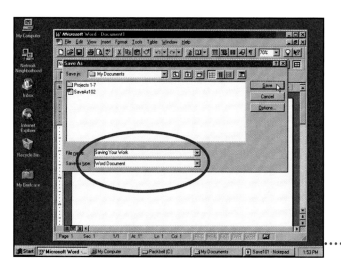

4 In the **File Name** text box, enter the name of the file you want to save. Use the filename **Saving Your Work**.

Puzzled?

For a quick save, click the button that has a floppy disk icon on the **Toolbar.** This will save your latest changes.

5 If you wanted to save a document as an older version file, you could change that as well. From the **Save as type** drop down list box, click the file type you desire. Save as type: **Word 2.X for Windows**.

Puzzled?

If for some reason, Word 2.x is not present in the file type selection box. You can always go back and install additional filters from your Word, Office CD, or disks. Another alternative is to save the document as a text file .TXT or rich text format .RTF.

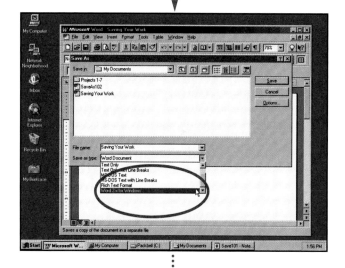

6 Once you have saved the correct name, location, and file type, choose the **Save** command button. The application saves the file and returns to the document window.

7 To save an existing document with a new name. On the **File** menu, choose **Save As**.

Missing Link

It is important to note that when working in a document, you can use the **Undo** command to reverse your choices.

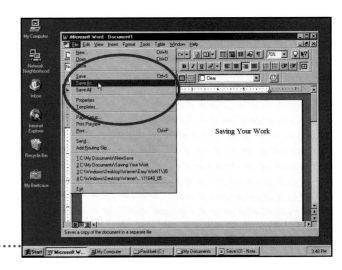

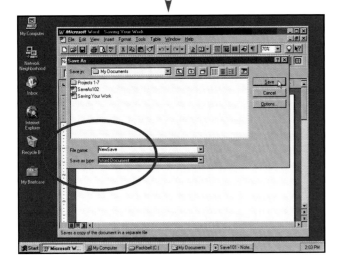

8 When the **Save As** window appears, type a new name in the **File Name** box. Let's use the file name **NewSave**. Lets also change the Save file type back to **Word Document** (the current version). Then, choose the **Save** command button.

Exiting an Application

"Why would I do this?"

When you are finished using an application or when you decide to end your computer session, you will need to exit the Windows NT applications you have opened. You can keep your applications open for later use, but this can sometimes use much of your computer's resources. This, in turn, can slow down other applications and processes you wish to use.

Task 29: Exiting an Application

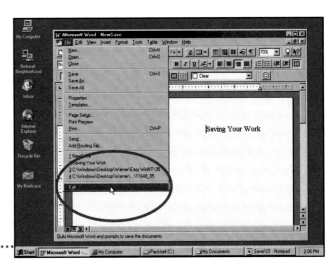

1 Make sure you have an application open, if not, please refer to Task 25, "Starting an Application with the Start Menu." To exit an application, open the application's **File** menu and choose the **Exit** command. Every Windows NT application works this way.

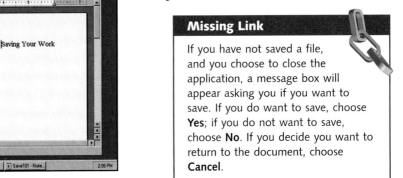

2 A second method of closing an application is to open the application's **Control** menu by clicking on the icon in the left corner of the title bar. From the **Control** menu, choose **Close**; alternatively, press **Alt+F4**.

Missing Link

If you have not saved a file, and you choose to close the application, a message box will appear asking you if you want to save. If you do want to save, choose **Yes**; if you do not want to save, choose **No**. If you decide you want to return to the document, choose **Cancel**.

3 The final method of closing an application is to click the **Close** button **(X)** in the upper right-hand corner of the title bar. ■

Adding and Using Shortcuts

"Why would I do this?"

A shortcut can be created anywhere to allow the quick opening of programs, folders, documents, and drives. For example, you can place shortcuts on your desktop, where you only have to double-click once to start an application, open a commonly used folder or document, or access your floppy drive. This eliminates having to open multiple menus and folders, or the Windows NT Explorer.

Task 30: Adding and Using Shortcuts

1 Insert a disk into the floppy drive. Open the **My Computer** window. Right-click the **Floppy** drive and drag it to the desktop, below the **My Briefcase** icon. Notice that the icon is ghosted and a box with an upward pointing arrow appears over the name.

> **Puzzled?**
>
> If you do not have a **Floppy** drive to use in this exercise, choose the **Control Panel** folder instead of the drive icon. The exercise will work exactly the same.

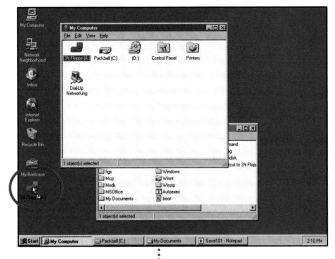

2 When you release the right mouse button, a quick menu will appear. You can either choose to **Create Shortcut Here** or **Cancel**. Choose **Create Shortcut Here** and the shortcut will appear on the desktop with "Shortcut to" added to the beginning of the icon's name.

> **Puzzled?**
>
> You might notice that the mouse pointer changes to a circle with a line through it while dragging the icon over the My Computer window. This is because this is not a location in which you can put a drive shortcut.

3 From the **Start** menu, choose the **Programs** command. Select **Windows NT Explorer**.

> **Puzzled?**
>
> If you are having problems with the Windows NT Explorer window, refer back to Task 23, "Using the Windows NT Explorer."

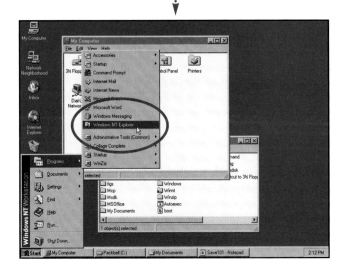

4 Locate the application you would like to create a shortcut of. We are going to try the **Microsoft Word** application. Right-click the **Word icon** and drag it to the desktop.

5 When you release the mouse button, you will get a quick menu asking if you want to Move, Copy, Create Shortcut Here, or Cancel. Choose **Create Shortcut Here** and the shortcut will appear on the desktop with "Shortcut to" added to the beginning of the icon's name.

6 To access the Floppy drive and Word application, double-click both of the shortcut icons on the desktop. The Floppy drive window will open and the Word application will start. Then, close the Word application and the Floppy drive with the **Close (X)** button. ■

95

Deleting Shortcuts

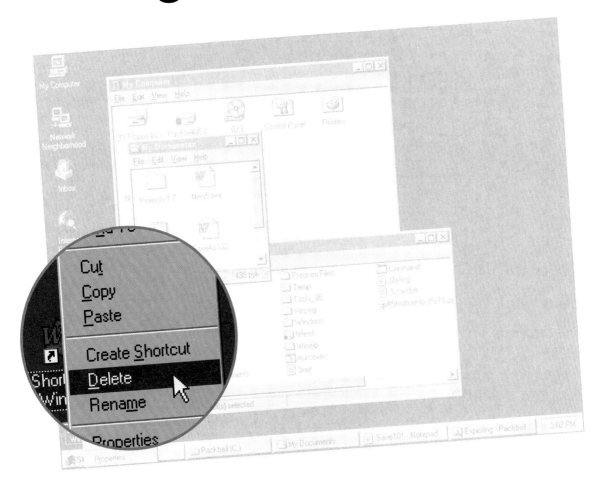

"Why would I do this?"

If you are not using a shortcut very often, you might simply want to remove the shortcut from your computer. This does not mean you want to remove the actual application, folder, file, or drive. You simply do not need the shortcut any longer. This task will show you how to delete a shortcut, much like you would delete any other file or folder.

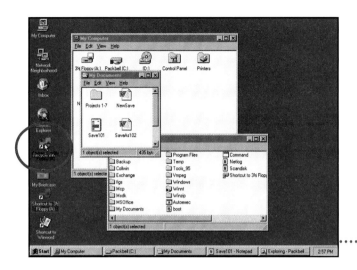

1 Select the **Floppy** drive shortcut by clicking once with the left mouse button on the icon. Drag the icon over the **Recycle Bin** icon. When the Recycle Bin icon changes to a darker color, release the **Floppy** drive shortcut.

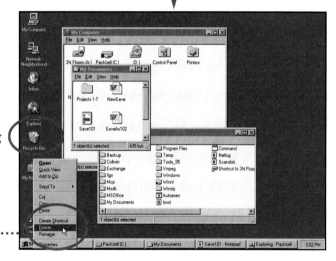

2 The Recycle Bin will appear as if there is trash in it. You can empty the Recycle Bin now or later. Refer to Task 20, "Using the Recycle Bin," for help on doing so. Another way to delete a shortcut is by right-clicking on the **Word** icon and selecting **Delete** from the quick menu to send the shortcut to the Recycle Bin.

3 A **Confirm File Delete** message box will appear asking you if you are sure you want to send the shortcut to the Recycle Bin. Choose the **Yes** button. ■

Puzzled?

If the shortcut you are deleting is a file on the network, it will not go to the recycle bin; it will be deleted outright.

Adding Items to the Start Menu

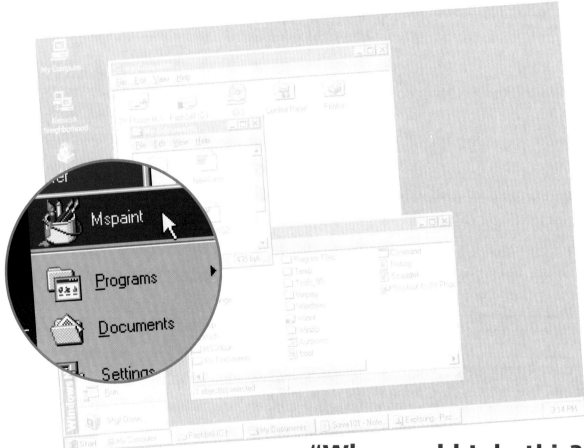

"Why would I do this?"

When you open your Start menu and access the different commands, you might find that there are certain commands you use more than others. For example, if you use Paint quite often, instead of opening up multiple secondary menus off the Start menu, why not place the command directly on the Start menu.

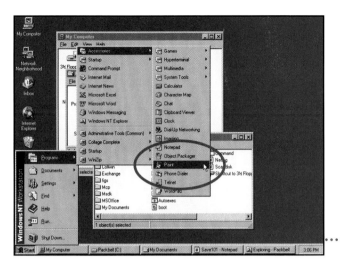

1 Open the **Start** menu and choose the **Programs** menu and then the **Accessories** Menu. Notice how many menus the Paint program is embedded in. We are going to make this program quicker to access from the Start menu.

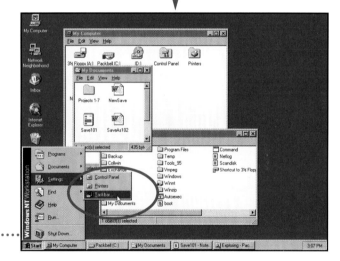

2 Open the **Start** menu and choose the **Settings** command. The **Settings** menu will appear. On the Settings menu, click **Taskbar**.

3 From the **Taskbar Properties** dialog box, click the **Start Menu Programs** tab. Click the **Add** button.

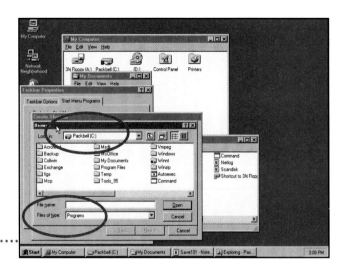

4 The **Create Shortcut** dialog box will appear. Click the **Browse** button to open the **Browse** window.

5 From the Browse window, locate the **Paint** program. Use the **Look in** drop down list box like you use the Windows NT Explorer. When you have found the program, either double-click it, or select it and click the **Open** button.

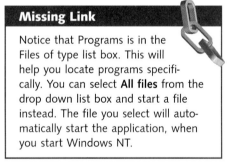

Missing Link

Notice that Programs is in the Files of type list box. This will help you locate programs specifically. You can select **All files** from the drop down list box and start a file instead. The file you select will automatically start the application, when you start Windows NT.

6 The **Create Shortcut** dialog box will appear again, but this time it will list the program you have selected, **Paint**. Click the **Next** button.

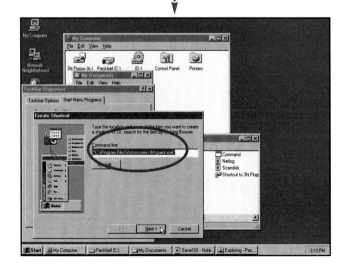

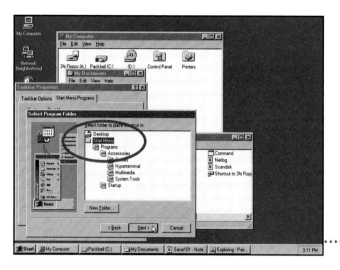

7 From the **Select Program Folder** dialog box, click the **Start Menu** folder. Click the **Next** button.

> **Puzzled?**
>
> You can choose other folders aside from the Start folder. It just depends on where you want to access the menu item.

8 The **Select a Title for the Program** dialog box will appear and you can type in any name you wish. Click the **Finish** button. If Windows NT asks you to choose an icon, click one and then click **Finish**. Choose **OK** in the **Taskbar Properties** dialog box to close it and return to the desktop.

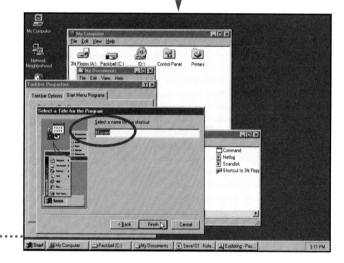

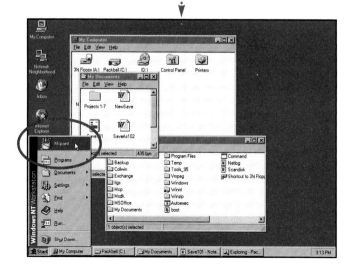

9 Now when you select the **Start** menu, there is an **MSPaint** command at the top. ■

> **Missing Link**
>
> Another quick way to add an item to the Start menu only is by dragging and dropping a file, folder, or program on top of the Start button in the Taskbar.

33

Deleting Items from the Start Menu

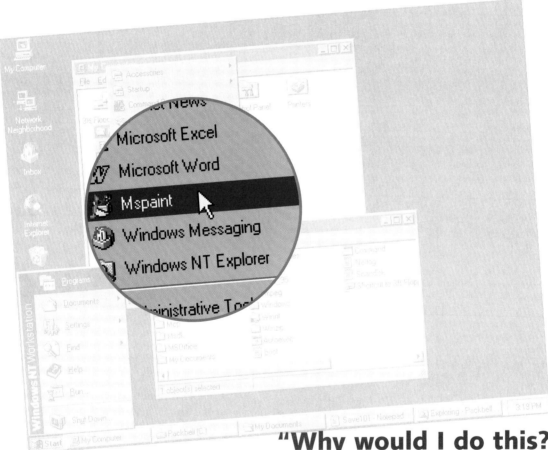

"Why would I do this?"

If you are not using a menu command very often, you might want to remove it from the menu. Or, you could simply move the command to a more remote location on one of your secondary menus. This task will show you how to delete a command or move the command to another menu.

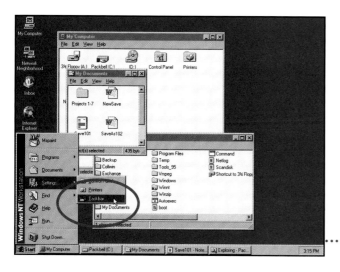

1 Open the **Start** menu and choose the **Settings** command. The **Settings** menu will appear. On the **Settings** menu, click **Taskbar**.

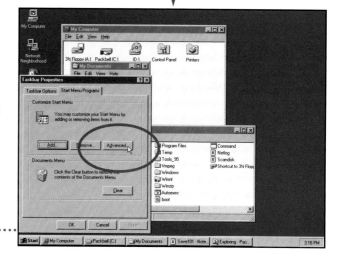

2 From the **Taskbar Properties** dialog box, click the **Start Menu Programs** tab. Choose the **Advanced** button.

3 An **Exploring** window will open and display the folders for the **Start Menu**. Click the **MSPaint** command (which is actually a small shortcut icon). While holding the left mouse button down, drag the MSPaint command to the folder you wish to move it to. We are going to choose the **Programs** folder. Then, **Close (X)** the **Exploring - Start Menu** window and choose the **OK** button in the **Taskbar Properties** dialog box.

4 Now when you open the **Start** menu and select the **Programs** command, you see the MSPaint command in the **Programs** menu instead of the **Start Menu**.

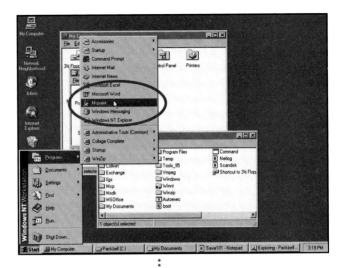

Puzzled?

If you decide you do not want to remove the item from the Start menu, close out of the Remove Shortcuts/Folders dialog box and Cancel out of the Start Menu Programs dialog box.

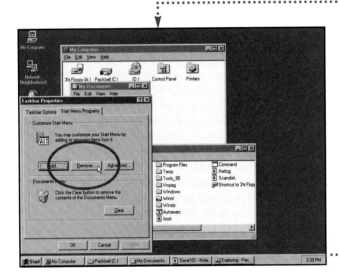

5 If you decide you want to delete a menu command from the **Programs** menu, select the **Start** menu, **Settings** menu, **Taskbar** command, **Start Menu Programs** tab (like in steps 1 and 2). This time click the **Remove** button.

6 From the **Remove Shortcuts/Folders** dialog box, choose the command you want to remove. We are going to remove the MSPaint application command. You might have to click some of the "**+**" to open folders and locate the command. Make sure you remember the title you selected for your command. Select **MSPaint** and click the **Remove** button.

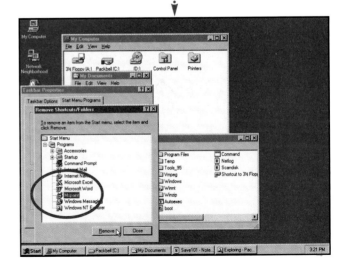

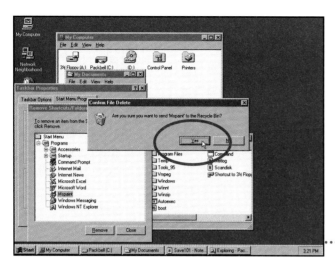

7 A **Confirm File Delete** message box will appear asking if you want to move the menu item to the Recycle Bin. Choose **Yes**. Choose the **Close** button in the **Remove Shortcuts/Folders** dialog box. Then choose the **OK** button on the **Taskbar Properties** dialog box.

8 Open the **Start**, **Programs** menu and you can see that the **Paint** application command has been removed. ■

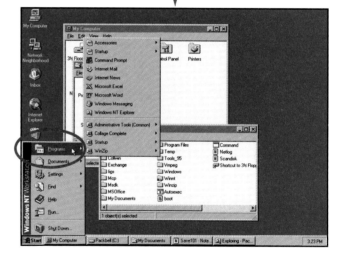

PART V

Printing with Windows NT

WHEN WINDOWS NT IS FIRST INSTALLED, the printer connected to your computer will automatically be configured. All Windows NT applications use the same configuration for your printer. This saves you time and ensures you can print from any Windows NT application without reconfiguring for each program. You can configure one or several printers to use with your computer, and you can switch between printers at any time. Additionally, you can easily manage printing for all your applications through Windows NT.

You print a document or graphic from an application in Windows NT, sometimes called a *print job*. For example, you create a marketing report in Microsoft Word that has Excel charts and Paint graphics. You can print that document from within Word.

Windows NT allows you to modify your print properties. Some of these properties are the paper source, paper size, and the page orientation. If you need the bottom tray of legal sized paper printed landscape, you can do it quickly and easily.

When you send that document to the printer, it first goes to a print *queue*. This queue is a line of files that a print spooler prints in the background while the computer performs other tasks in the foreground. This is why you can send a print job and then go on working in Windows NT.

Windows NT creates a print queue for each printer that is connected to your computer. You can even view the print jobs you have sent to each printer in their own separate queues.

You might have sent more than one document to be printed; thus, more than one file is in the print queue. Windows NT allows you control over the files in the print queue. While a file is in a print queue, you can manipulate the printer. You can pause the printer, perhaps to change paper. Then, you can restart the printer, to continue printing. If you find an error in the file you just printed, you can cancel the print job, correct the mistake, and print the document again.

Windows NT also enables you to easily change printer settings, such as the printer port and drivers. Additionally, you can change the print tray, memory, and the fonts that are installed on your printer. You can even print a test page from Windows NT to see if your printer is set up correctly.

In addition to managing the print queue and printer settings, Windows NT enables you to easily add printers to your computer by using a step-by-step guide called a Wizard. The Wizard guides you through installing the hardware and any drivers that may come with your printer.

When you have two or more printers attached to your computer and configured in Windows NT, you can choose one of the printers to be the *default*. The default printer is the one that you commonly use and that your applications will print to unless otherwise directed.

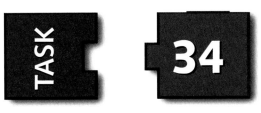

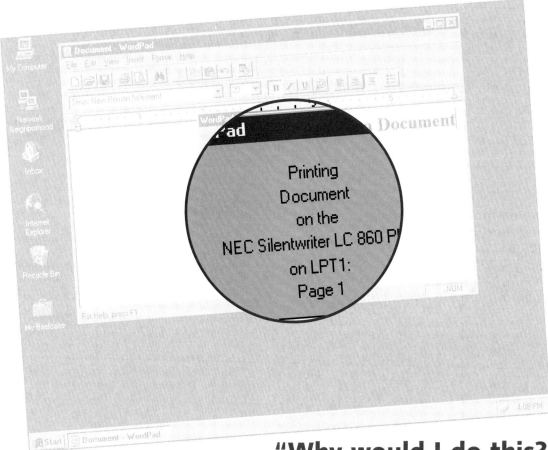

Printing a Document

"Why would I do this?"

You can print documents from any Windows NT applications like WordPad or Paint, or even from application that have been installed like Microsoft Word, Adobe Illustrator, Claris WordPerfect, or others. Printing gives you a hard copy that you can use to read, give to co-workers, mail, fax, or file. Additionally, due to Windows NT's multitasking capabilities, once you send a file to print, you can continue on with other work you have to do in Windows NT.

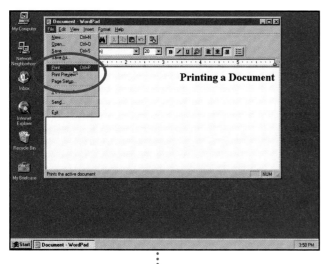

1 Open a Windows NT application, like **WordPad**. From the **File** menu, choose the **Print** command. The application may also provide a shortcut key combination like **Ctrl+P**.

Missing Link

To print immediately, you can click the toolbar button that has a printer icon, without changing the print options. You will print with the settings last entered into the Print dialog box.

2 The **Print** dialog box opens. In the **Printer** section of **Print** dialog box, the name of the printer you are currently using will be listed in the **Name** text box. If you wish to change your printer, see Task 39, "Changing Printer Settings." If you wish to change print properties, like orientation and type of paper, see Task 35, "Modifying Print Properties." You are going to choose to print one copy of all pages. Choose **OK** to print the document.

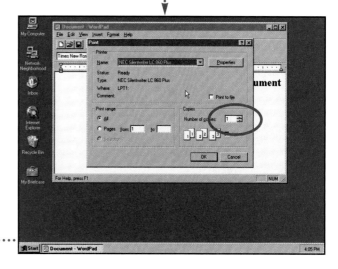

3 The Print dialog box closes, and the document is sent to your printer and a message dialog box appears to tell you that your document is printing. If you need to cancel the printing for any reason, you can click the **Cancel** button here. ■

Missing Link

If you want to change your printer, paper size, page orientation, or specifics about printing graphics, see Task 35, "Modifying Print Properties."

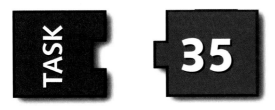

Modifying Print Properties

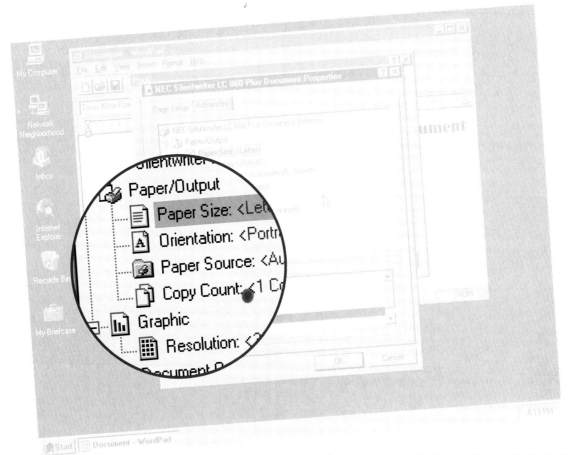

"Why would I do this?"

There are numerous types of printer settings that you can change. You can change the orientation of your letter–size paper from portrait (8.5" × 11") to landscape (11" × 8.5"), change the size of your paper (letter to legal), enhance your graphics (75 dpi to 300 dpi), and much more. This task will show you how to modify your print properties so that your printout looks like what you see on-screen.

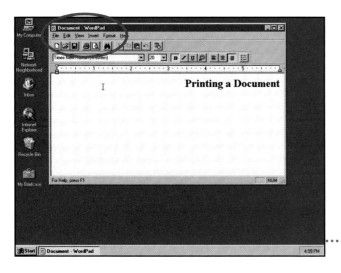

1 Open the **WordPad** application. If you already have it open, click once on the **WordPad** title bar to make it the active window.

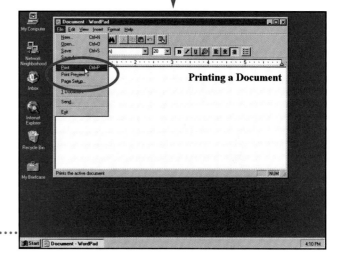

2 From the **File** menu, choose the **Print** command.

3 Once the **Print** dialog box appears, choose the **Properties** button.

4 Choose the **Page Setup** tab to modify the paper size (legal or letter), paper source (upper or lower tray), number of copies, and the page orientation (portrait or landscape).

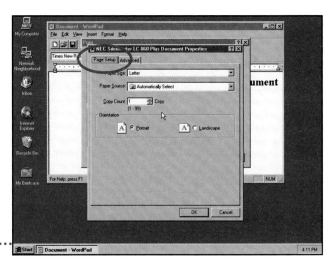

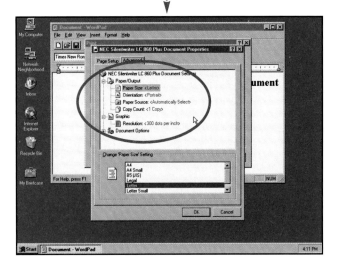

5 From the **Advanced** tab you can modify the paper size, source, copies, and orientation in a hierarchical view. In addition, you can change your graphics resolution for a more or less dense printout. (The higher the number of dots per inch "dpi" the more dense the printout, the better the graphics resolution.) Once you have made your modifications, choose the **OK** button. Then, choose the **OK** button on the Print dialog box and your document will print with the new settings. ∎

Missing Link

If you make a change in the Print tabs, the properties remain changed until you exit and reopen the application, or until you modify them again.

Viewing the Print Queue

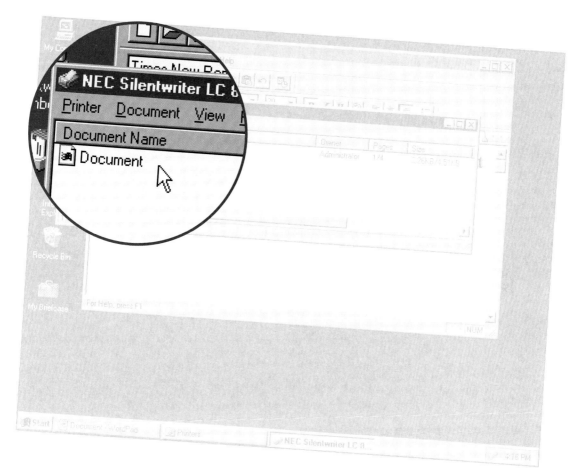

"Why would I do this?"

The print queue lists the documents that you have sent to a printer. This queue lets you know the status of your print job. It might be finished, waiting to be printed, or currently being printed. This task shows you how to view the print queue.

1 Open the **Start** menu and choose **Settings**. A secondary menu appears. From the secondary menu, choose **Printers**. From the **Printers** window, double-click the printer whose print queue you want to view. The printer window opens with a list of the documents in the queue plus statistics about the documents being printed. If the window is empty, there is nothing in the print queue. (Your print job might already be finished.)

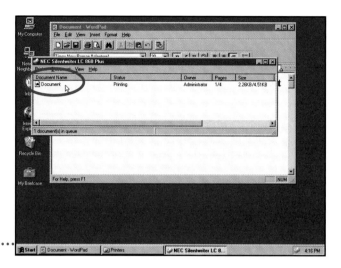

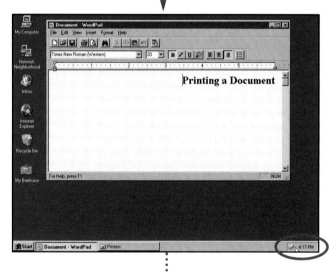

Puzzled?

Your printer will have the same name as it was in the Name drop down list box from the Print dialog box, in Task 34, "Printing a Document."

2 A shortcut to the printer print queue is to double-click the **Printer** icon in the system tray, in the lower right-hand corner of the desktop, on the taskbar. This icon will only show up if you have sent a print job recently and it is not finished printing.

3 To close the print queue, click the **Close** button **(X)** in the window's title bar. ■

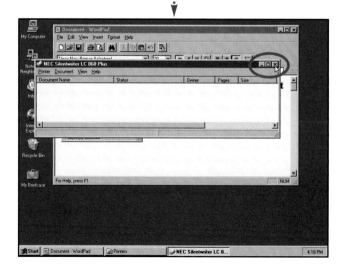

Pausing and Restarting the Printer

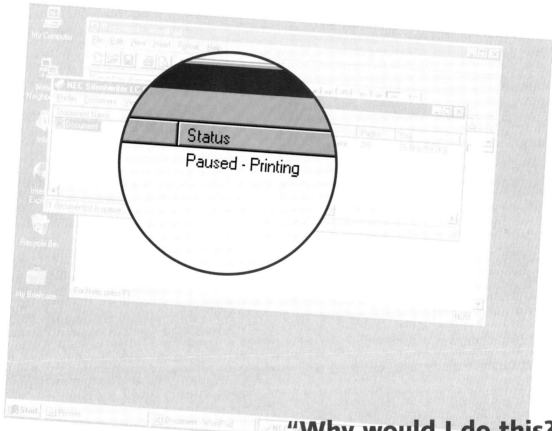

"Why would I do this?"

Have you ever printed a document, then remembered that you wanted to use company logo paper? If the document has not started printing yet, you can pause the print job, change the paper, and restart the print queue. Using the print queue, you can pause or restart your print jobs.

1 After sending a print job to the printer, open the print queue window from Task 36, "Viewing the Print Queue." (Double-click the **Printer** icon in the system tray.) In the print queue window, open the **Printer** menu and choose **Pause Printing**. This will add a check mark to the **Pause Printing** command, signifying that it is the current status.

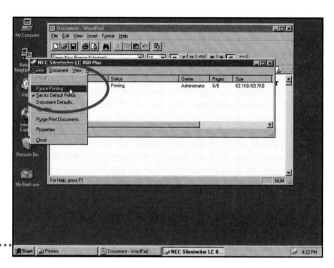

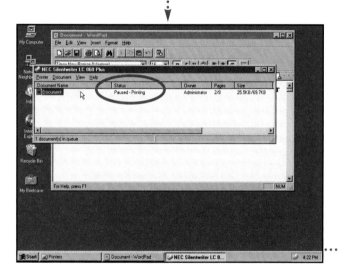

2 Notice in the print queue window, the **Status** of the document is **Paused - Printing**.

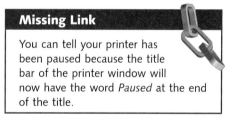

Missing Link

You can tell your printer has been paused because the title bar of the printer window will now have the word *Paused* at the end of the title.

3 To restart the printing of a paused job, open the **Printer** menu and choose **Pause Printing** again. This will remove the check mark and resume printing. ■

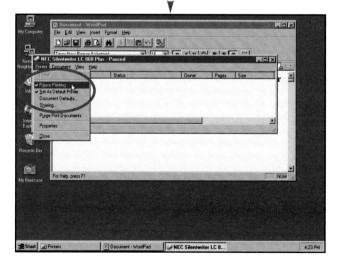

Canceling Printing

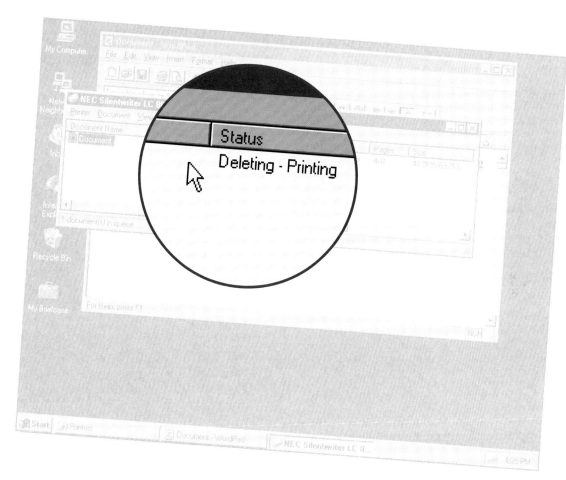

"Why would I do this?"

Have you ever printed a document and then noticed on-screen that there is a typo? If your printer has not printed the page, you can cancel the print job. Canceling the print job can save you time and paper.

1 After sending a print job to the printer, open the print queue window from Task 36, "Viewing the Print Queue." (Double-click the Printer icon in the system tray.) In the print queue window, select the print job you want to cancel, right-click with the mouse, and from the quick menu choose **Cancel**.

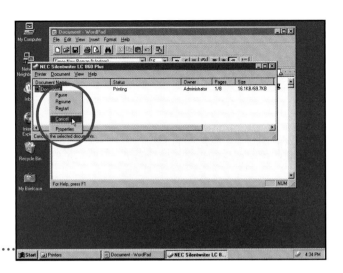

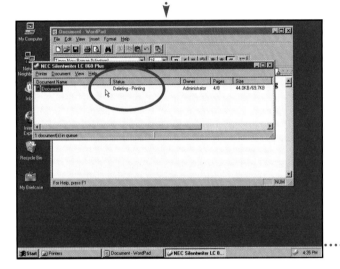

2 Notice in the print queue window, the **Status** of the document is **Deleting - Printing**.

3 If you want all the print jobs cancelled that you have sent, you can select the **Printer** menu and choose the **Purge Print Documents** command. They will all be removed from the print queue. ■

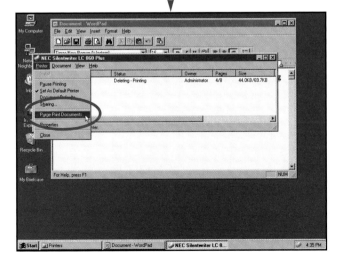

Changing Printer Settings

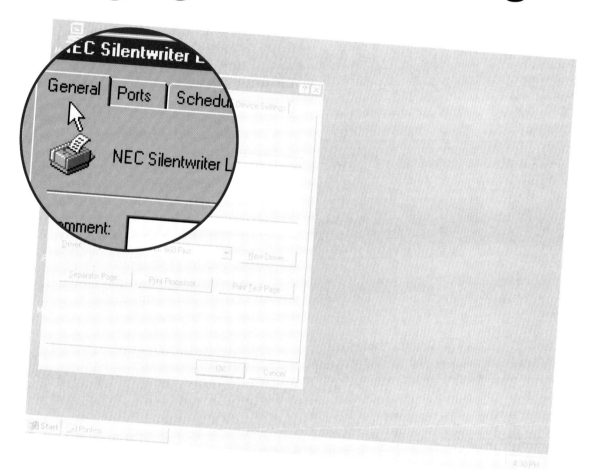

"Why would I do this?"

Printer settings enable you to modify the way your printer is set up and thus the way the printer responds to all your Windows NT applications. This task will show you the most common settings that you will ever need to modify.

Task 39: Changing Printer Settings

1 Open the **Start** menu and choose **Settings**. A secondary menu appears. From the secondary menu, choose **Printers**.

Missing Link

Changing the printer's properties changes all documents you print. If you want to change properties for just one document, use the **Page Settings** or **Print Setup** command in the particular program.

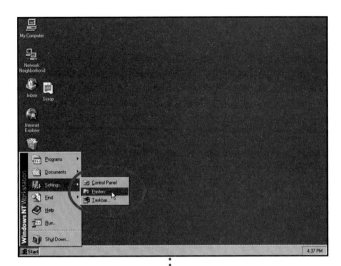

2 From the **Printers** window, click once on the printer for which you want to change settings. Open the **File** menu and choose **Properties**.

3 The **Printer's Properties** dialog box will appear with various tabs that enable you to change settings. Choose the **General** tab to change the printer drivers and to print a test page.

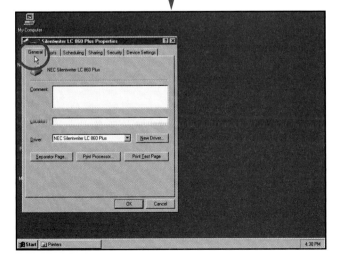

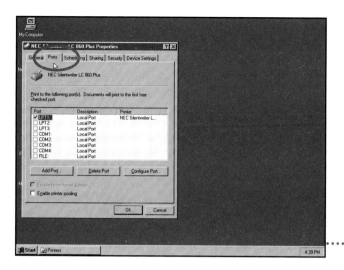

4 Choose the **Ports** tab to change or add a printer port.

5 For now, the only other tab that you need to know about is the **Device Settings** tab. This tab lets you change the print tray, the printer memory, and the fonts that are installed for your printer. More information on scheduling, sharing, and security are in Part VI, "Sharing Resources with Windows NT." Once you have changed the printer settings that you want, choose the **OK** button. This will save your changes. You can now close the **Printers** window by clicking the **(X)**. ■

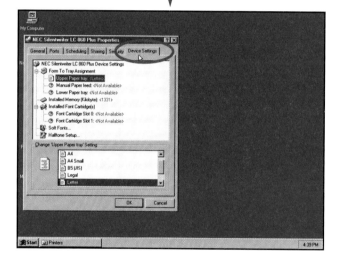

TASK 40

Adding a Printer

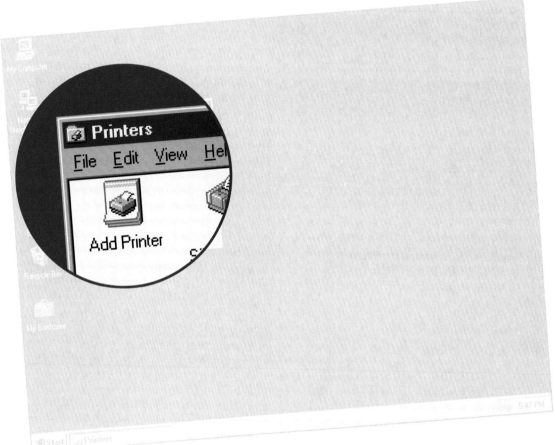

"Why would I do this?"

You can add a new printer to your Windows NT configuration using a step-by-step guide that Windows NT provides, called a Wizard. Use the Wizard when you get a new printer, change printers, or want to attach to a different printer.

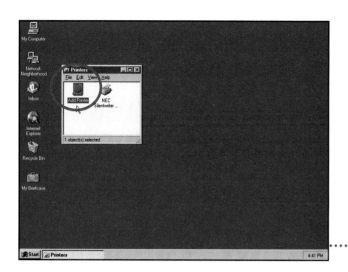

1 Open the **Start** menu, choose the **Settings** command, and select the **Printers** command. In the **Printers Folder** window, double-click the **Add Printer** icon.

2 The first dialog box of the **Add Printer Wizard** appears. Choose whether you are going to add your own printer, or a network printer. Choose **Next** button to continue with the installation of the new printer.

Missing Link

If you wish to cancel out of the Add Printer Wizard at any time, select the **Cancel** button.

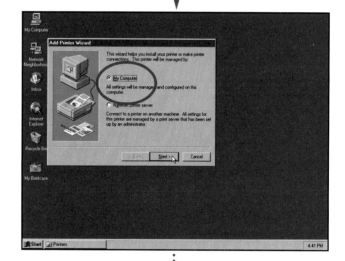

3 The second **Add Printer Wizard** dialog box appears. Choose the port for the connection of the printer by clicking once on the appropriate box, **LPT1:** for example, and click the **Next** button.

Puzzled?

If the printer you want to add is on a network, you would select **Network** printer. Follow the directions on-screen for the rest of the wizard boxes.

4 The third **Add Printer Wizard** dialog box appears. Choose the **Manufacturers** name and select the **Printers** name. You can choose the **Have Disk** button and use the manufacturers disk to load the drivers, or you can choose **Next** and Windows NT will prompt you for the disk or CD to load its own drivers.

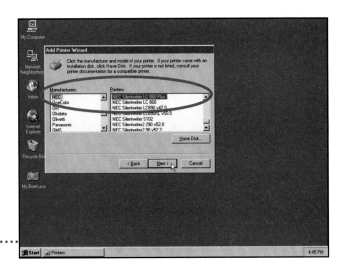

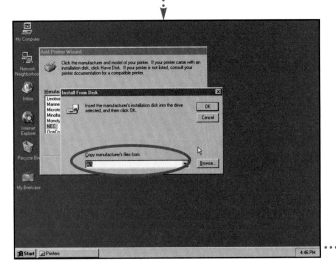

5 If you choose to use a Windows NT driver for the new printer, Windows NT prompts you for the disk or CD. Insert the disk or CD and enter the path in the copy files from the text box. Choose **OK** to continue adding the printer.

6 The next **Add Printer Wizard** dialog box appears only if you have installed that printer before. If you are installing a printer for the first time, you will not get this dialog box. In the **Add Printer Wizard** dialog box, you are asked whether you want to keep your existing driver or replace it. We will choose to keep the existing driver. Choose **Next**.

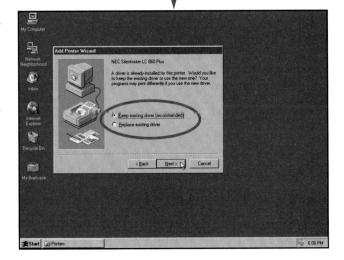

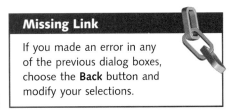

Missing Link

If you made an error in any of the previous dialog boxes, choose the **Back** button and modify your selections.

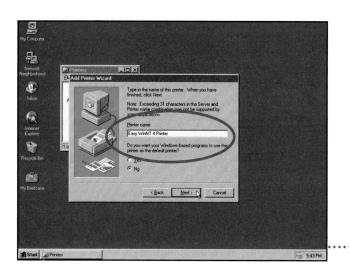

7 The next **Add Printer Wizard** dialog box appears. Enter a name for the printer—you can name the printer anything you like)—or accept the one Windows NT has given it. You will also need to decide if you want the new printer to be the default printer. For now, choose the **No** radio button. We will discuss how to assign a default printer next, in Task 41. Choose **Next** when you finish.

8 The next **Add Printer Wizard** dialog box appears. Choose whether you want the printer to be shared or not. We will cover more on printer sharing in Part VI, "Sharing Resources with Windows NT." For now, select the radio button **Not shared**. Choose the **Next** button.

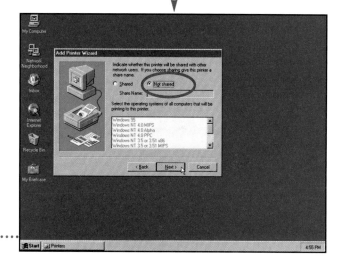

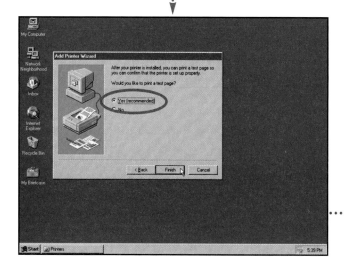

9 When the final **Add Printer Wizard** dialog box appears, choose to print a test page by selecting the **Yes** radio button. Click the **Finish** button.

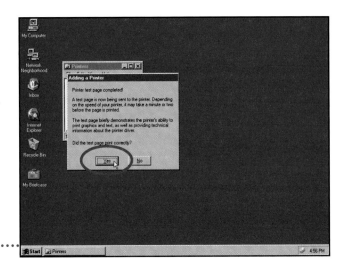

10 Windows displays a message box telling you it printed the test page, and then asking if it printed successfully. Choose **Yes** if it did.

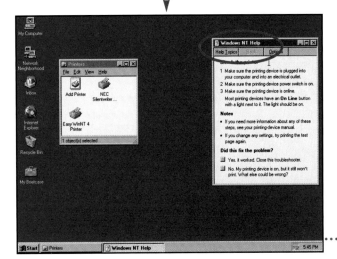

11 If it did not print successfully, choose **No**, and Windows NT will take you to Windows NT Help, where it will give you problems to check for.

12 You can now see the new Printer icon in the Printer folder. ■

Missing Link

If you want to delete a printer, simply right-click the appropriate printer icon in the Printer folder and choose **Delete**. You will get a message box asking whether you want to delete the printer. If you do, select **Yes**. The printer will be removed, and you will no longer have it available; if you don't, select **No** and the printer will still be available.

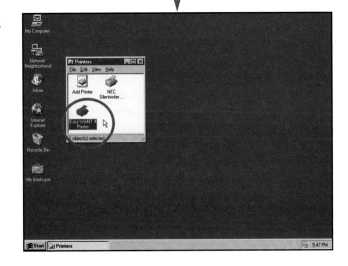

Setting the Default Printer

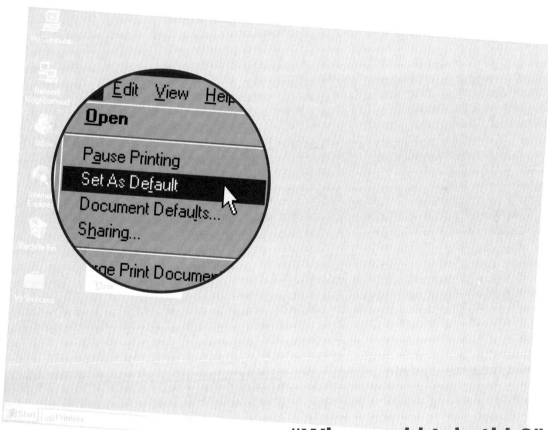

"Why would I do this?"

If your computer is connected to a network printer along with a printer of your own, you can choose the one you want to be your default printer. If you would rather your documents automatically be printed to your personal printer, this task shows you how to set the default printer in Windows NT.

Task 41: Setting the Default Printer

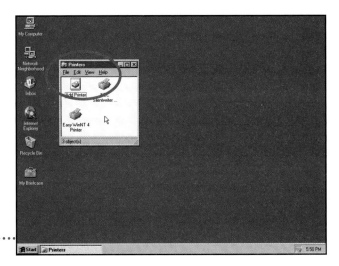

1 Your Printers window should still be open. If it is not, open the **Start** menu and choose **Settings**. A secondary menu appears. From the secondary menu, choose **Printers**.

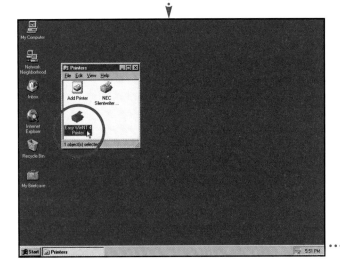

2 From the **Printers** window, select the printer you want to choose as your default printer.

3 Choose **File**, **Set As Default**. Look at the File menu again and you will see a check mark to the left of the Set As Default command. This will appear whenever you select that particular printer and open the File menu. ■

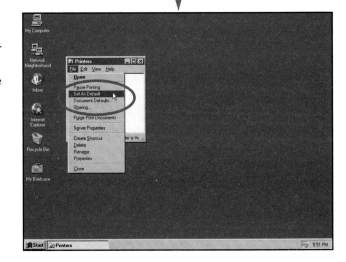

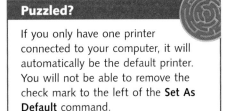

Puzzled?

If you only have one printer connected to your computer, it will automatically be the default printer. You will not be able to remove the check mark to the left of the **Set As Default** command.

PART VI

Sharing Resources with Windows NT

A computer that is networked is not necessarily a resource that can be used by others. You must select which files or resources you wish to share on your network. This prevents others from accessing files that you want to keep secure. In order for you to access other shared resources, you need to learn how to locate a computer, find the folder(s), or access the printer that you need. If you have any trouble finding a specific shared resource, there are applications in Windows NT that will help you.

If you have data on your hard drive that someone else needs, it may be more convenient to share the resource on your hard drive that contains this data. Then, users could access the data as a shared resource.

Last, but not least, there may come a time when you need to change the workgroup or domain that your computer belongs to. For example, you move to the Sales department, but still want to access the color printer in the Marketing department. You will learn how to do this and more in the following tasks.

COMPUTERS, PRINTERS, FOLDERS, and other resources can be shared across a network. It is an easy way to quickly access resource on a local network. You use Microsoft's Network Neighborhood to connect to other computers. This eliminates the need to map drive letters, as you might have had to do in the past. Instead of mapping drive letters, the name of the computer is used to access its resources.

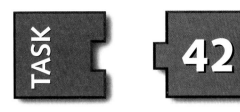

TASK 42

Network Neighborhood

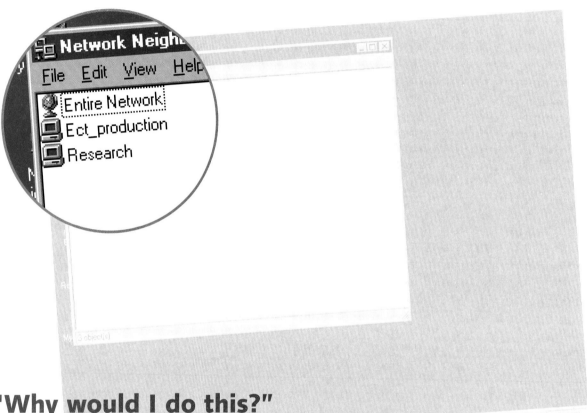

"Why would I do this?"

The Network Neighborhood is a Microsoft analogy for the network resources that are located within a computer network. It is an easy way to quickly access resources on a local network. You may use Network Neighborhood to take advantage of departmental printers, file servers, or data located on a coworker's machine. Using Network Neighborhood to connect to other computers also eliminates the need to map drive letters. Instead of mapping drive letters, the name of the computer is used to access its resources.

For many tasks, it may only be necessary to access resources located on a local or departmental network. Most of the time, these resources will be allocated so that they appear immediately within the Network Neighborhood. However, if resources are needed that reside on another network or even another type of network, they can be accessed by browsing the entire network to locate remote resources. An example might be searching for accounting information on a computer in New York from a Windows NT network in Indianapolis.

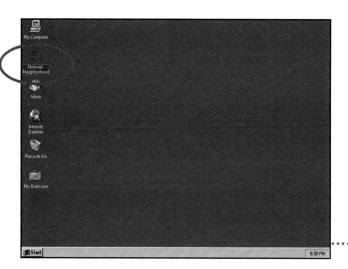

1 Double-click the **Network Neighborhood** icon on your desktop.

2 The **Network Neighborhood** window appears. There will be a globe icon named Entire Network. Depending on the network setup of your computer, there may be other icons in this window.

Missing Link

The icons in the Network Neighborhood represent different resources. A single computer represents an individual computer. Several computers pictured together represent a workgroup, domain, or some other network grouping. An icon that appears to be several wires connected together represents a network operating system. In addition, network printing resources are represented by a printer icon.

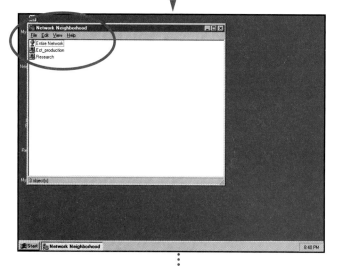

3 Open the Windows NT Explorer (see Task 23) and you will also see that the Network Neighborhood can be accessed through its desktop representation from the Windows NT Explorer. ■

133

TASK

43

Linking to Another Network

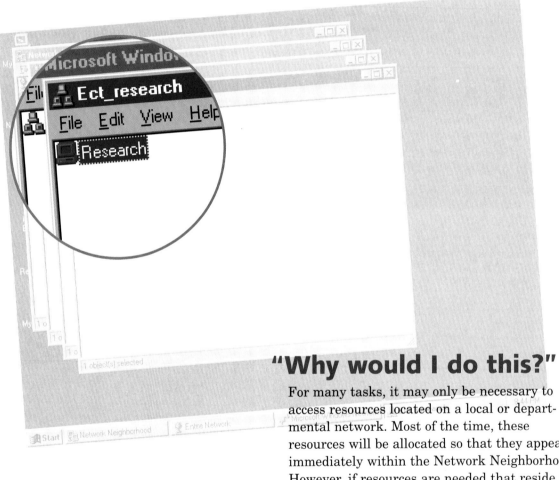

"Why would I do this?"

For many tasks, it may only be necessary to access resources located on a local or departmental network. Most of the time, these resources will be allocated so that they appear immediately within the Network Neighborhood. However, if resources are needed that reside on another network or even another type of network, they can be accessed by browsing the entire network to locate remote resources. An example might be searching for accounting information on a Netware server in New York from a Windows NT network in Indianapolis.

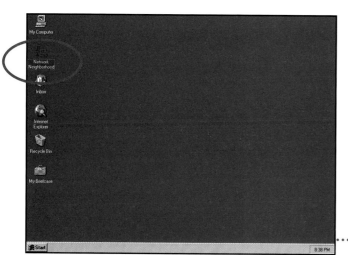

1 Double-click the **Network Neighborhood** icon on your desktop.

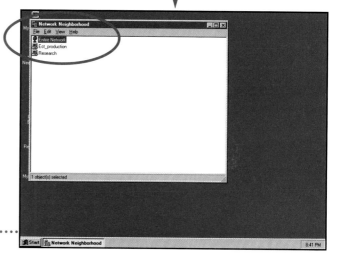

2 In the **Network Neighborhood** window, double-click the **Entire Network** icon.

3 The **Entire Network** window will appear. Depending on the network setup of your computer you will see one or more network icons representing different types of network operating systems. Double-click the **Microsoft Windows Network** icon.

Task 43: Linking to Another Network

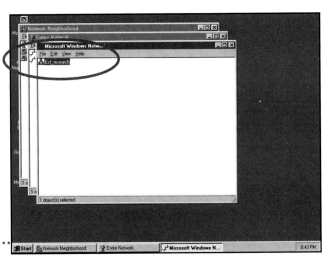

4 The **Microsoft Windows Network** window will open and list the workgroups and domains that are available to your computer. Double-click a **domain** in the Microsoft Windows Network window.

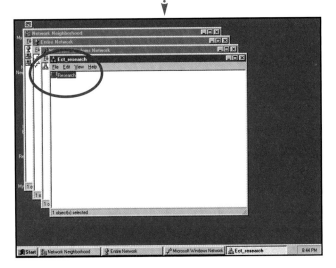

5 A window will appear that shows the computers in the selected workgroup or domain. This window could be empty if their are no shared resources or you do not have access to any resources within the selected workgroup or domain. ■

Missing Link

Another quick way to explore shared resources is to click the Start button, choose the Run command, and type **computer** or **computer\share** in the list box. This will allow you to browse the network resource without knowing the exact resource name.

Puzzled?

Workgroups and domains are very similar. Both are groupings of computers. Both use Microsoft Networking. Both can make resource available to others using Microsoft Networking. The difference is that anyone can create a workgroup, join a workgroup, or use the shared resources of a workgroup. Domains can only be created using a Windows NT Server and not anyone can use a domain's resources. A computer designated as a primary domain controller keeps a list of users who may access the domain's resources and which shared resources the users are allowed to use.

Computers and Folders

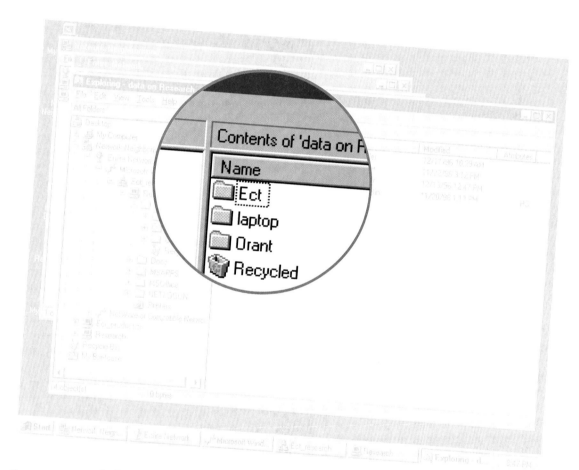

"Why would I do this?"

A networked computer by itself is not a resource that can be used. The computer must contain shared resources. After locating a computer, you must find the folder, folders, or printer that you need the use of. In other words, now that you have found the server in New York, you must find the folder that contains the accounting information you need.

137

1 From the domain window that was opened in Step 5 of Task 43, double-click one of the **computers**.

2 A window opens that lists the shared resources of the computer you selected.

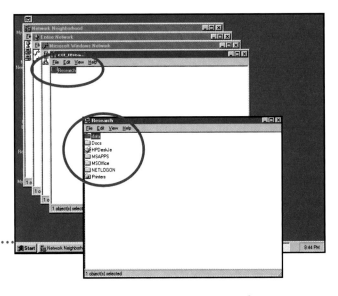

Missing Link

Shared resources might be data or peripherals located on other computers. Remember, that these shared resources are located on computers that are utilized by many users. Any changes that you make to shared data affects everyone who uses that data.

3 To quickly view the contents of one of these folders, right-click a **folder** and choose **Explore** from the shortcut menu.

4 A **Windows NT Explorer** window opens with the tree view of the resources on the left expanded to the folder that you just selected and the contents listed on the right. ■

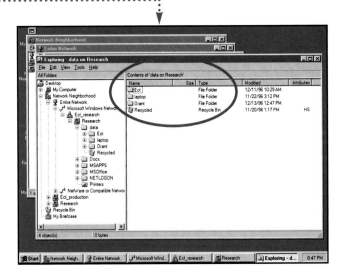

Finding Shared Resources

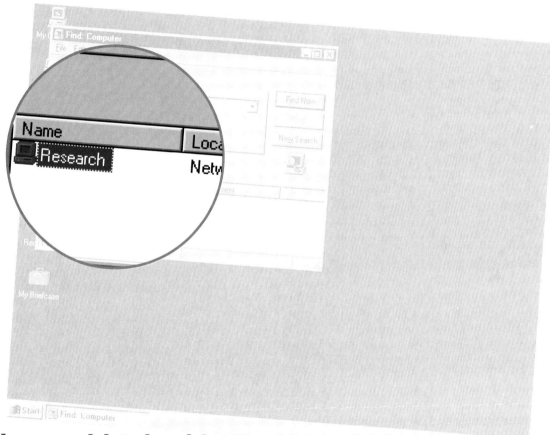

"Why would I do this?"

On a large network, there will be many
resources. At times, it may be difficult to locate
a particular resource on your network.
However, if you know the name of the computer
that contains the resource you are looking for,
you can use the Find Computer utility. After
supplying a computer name, Windows NT
searches all available networks for a computer
identified by the name supplied. This saves the
time of manually looking through many different domains or workgroups.

1 From the **Start** menu, select the **Find** command. From the **Find** menu, choose the **Computer** command.

Puzzled?

You may wonder why the Find Computer dialog box uses a drop down list box to allow the entry of a computer name to search for. This is done because previous entries are listed and can be viewed by opening the drop down list box. This could save the time of typing a long name that was searched for previously.

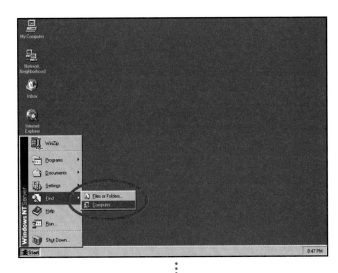

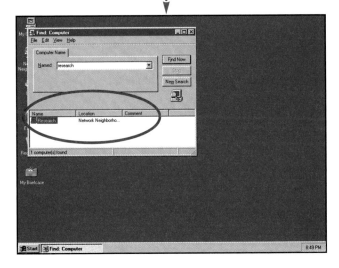

2 The **Find Computer** dialog box appears. It has a single edit box that allows you to enter a name to search for. If you know the **name** of your computer, enter it in the **Find Computer** dialog box. Otherwise, leave the entry blank. Then, choose the **Find Now** button.

Missing Link

Leaving the entry blank in the Find Computer dialog box will search for any shared computer on the network and list it in the bottom portion of the dialog.

3 Any computers that match the criteria you supplied will be listed in the bottom portion of the dialog box. Computers in this list can be accessed just as computers were accessed in Task 44. ■

Sharing Resources

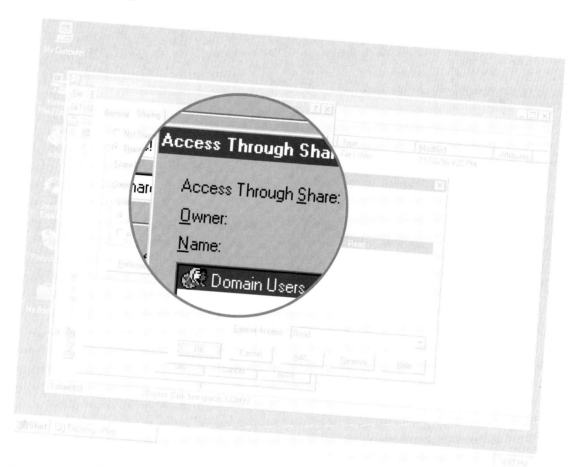

"Why would I do this?"

There could be data that you have on your hard drive that someone else needs. If this data changes frequently, it may be impractical to constantly copy to a server or floppy disk for the other person. In this case, you could share the resource on your hard drive that contains this data. Then, users could access the data as a shared resource.

1 From the **Start** menu, select the **Programs** command. From the **Programs** menu, choose the **Windows NT Explorer** command.

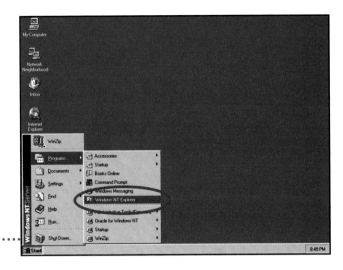

2 When the **Windows NT Explorer** window opens, expand the **Program Files** folder and select any folder. We are going to choose the **Plus! Folder**.

3 From the **File** menu choose the **Properties** command.

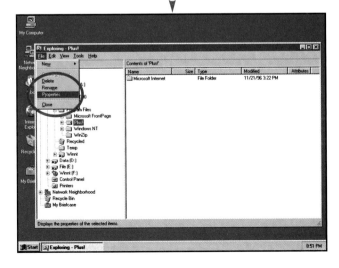

4 The **Plus! Properties** dialog opens and displays the **General** page. Select the **Sharing** page by clicking the tab labeled **Sharing**.

> **Missing Link**
>
> In addition, you may see a Security tab on the Plus! Properties dialog box. This tab will be there if your hard disk or partition with the Plus! Directory is formatted with Windows NT File System (NTFS).

5 The **Sharing** page indicates that this folder is not shared.

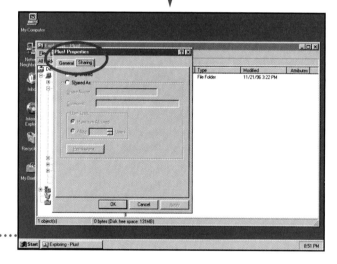

6 Select the **Shared As** radio button. By default, the **Share Name** will be the name of the resource being shared but this can be changed. Enter an appropriate **comment** and then choose the **Permissions** button.

7 The **Access Through Share Permissions** dialog is displayed. By default, this shared resource can be accessed by **Everyone** on your network. In addition, any user can make a change or even delete files within this folder. Press the **Remove** button to do away with the default permission.

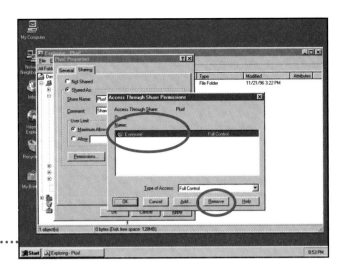

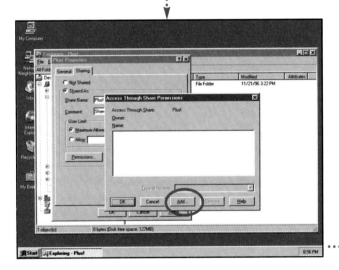

8 The **Everyone** permission has been removed. Now choose the **Add** button to add a new permission.

9 The **Add Users and Groups** dialog appears. Select **Domain Users** in the Names list and select the **Read** option in the Type of Access drop down list box. When finished choose the **Add** button.

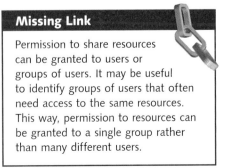

Missing Link

Permission to share resources can be granted to users or groups of users. It may be useful to identify groups of users that often need access to the same resources. This way, permission to resources can be granted to a single group rather than many different users.

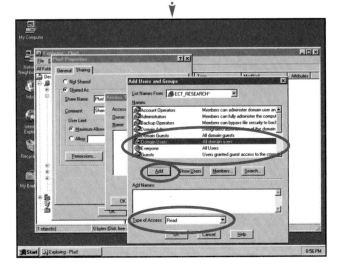

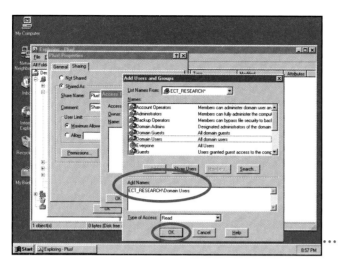

10 The **Names** that you select appear in the **Add Names** list. After adding all of the users or groups necessary, choose the **OK** button.

11 Now, the users or groups you selected and the type of access they are allowed are listed in the **Permissions** dialog box. Press the **OK** button in the **Permissions** dialog box and the **Properties** dialog box.

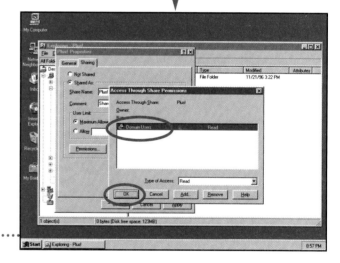

12 The **Plus! Folder** should now look as if there is a hand holding the bottom of the folder. This is how a shared resource is indicated graphically. ■

145

TASK

47

Changing Workgroups or Domains

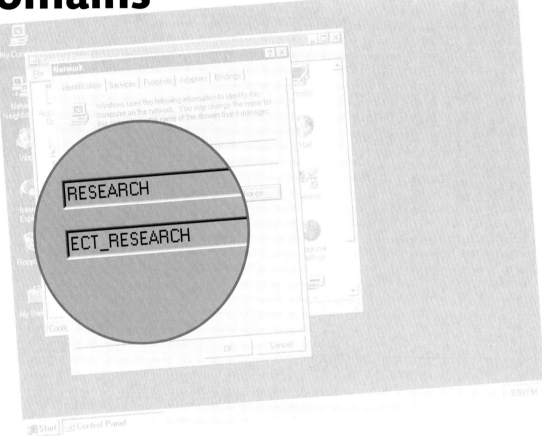

"Why would I do this?"

If you are moved to a different department or
receive a computer from a different department,
you may need to change the workgroup or
domain that the computer belongs to.

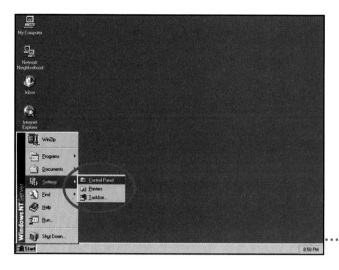

1 From the **Start** menu select the **Settings** command. From the **Settings** menu choose the **Control Panel** command.

2 Once the **Control Panel** window is open, double-click the **Network** icon.

Puzzled?

If you join a workgroup, but still can't see your computer listed in that workgroup, check your spelling of the workgroup name. When joining a workgroup, the spelling is not checked and a misspelling will result in the creation of a new workgroup.

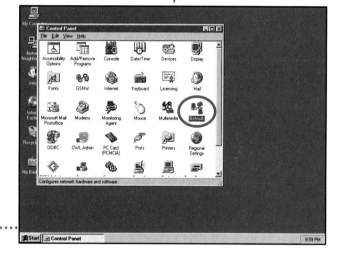

3 When the **Network** dialog appears, it will display the **Identification** page. This contains the **Computer Name** and either the workgroup or domain. Press the **Change** button.

4 Enter in the **Workgroup** or **Domain** that you want to belong to, type in the correct **Username** and **Password**, and choose the **OK** button. ■

Missing Link

When assigning a computer to a domain, be sure to use a valid username and password. Otherwise, the attempt to join the domain will fail.

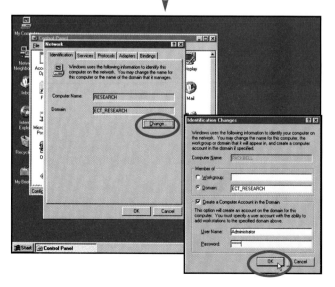

147

PART VII

Accessing the Internet Using Windows NT

WINDOWS NT PROVIDES ACCESS to network facilities such as electronic mail, web browsing, and file downloading. While you can purchase software to accomplish these tasks, all the tools necessary to utilize these functions are provided with Windows NT. The network access is provided either by a network that you are directly connected to, or by a network that you connect to using a modem and a phone line.

Dial-up networking is provided to allow NT workstations to call other computers, and use the other computer's network. In many cases, the other computer's network is connected to the Internet, but it doesn't have to be. Once connected, Windows NT can use resources on the other network as if they were directly connected to the workstation. Depending on the speed of your phone connection, network tasks over this type of connection could take longer to complete.

One of the more powerful network tools is electronic mail or e-mail. E-mail can be used to send text messages and even sound or video messages. These messages can be sent to a single person or several people at the same time. The Windows messaging system provided with Windows NT can be used to connect to a server, using an e-mail account to send or receive e-mail messages.

The latest and possibly the most powerful network tool is the Web Server. A web server is a computer that serves, or provides, web pages. Web pages can be static, dynamic, or even interactive. Opportunities for use are nearly endless for web pages and their abilities continue to grow at a rapid pace.

48

Dial-Up Networking

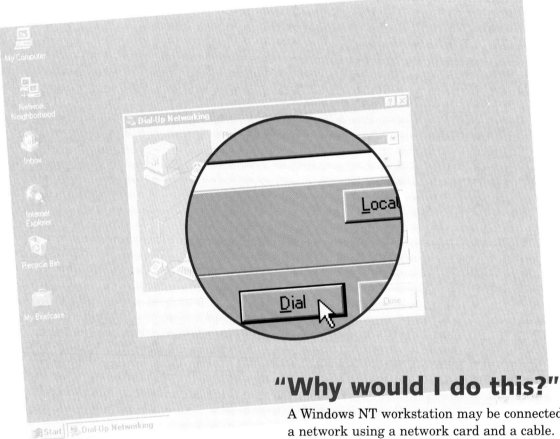

"Why would I do this?"

A Windows NT workstation may be connected to a network using a network card and a cable. This direct network connection may or may not provide access to services such as e-mail and web servers or to the Internet. If a network does not provide this access, or does not provide to an appropriate system, then dial-up networking can be used to call another network. This call creates a network connection over a phone line that can be used just as the direct network connection is. However, the connection will be much slower.

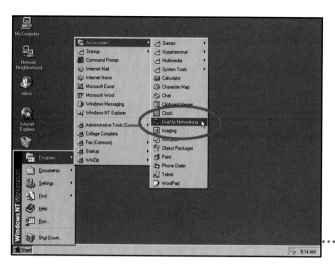

1 Open the **Start** menu and choose the **Programs** command. From the **Programs** menu, choose the **Accessories** folder. From the **Accessories** menu, choose the **Dial-Up Networking** command.

2 If this is the first time your computer has used Dial-Up Networking, a message box will alert you of this fact. The message box will also ask that you press **OK** to add a phonebook entry. Otherwise, a **Dial-Up Networking** dialog box will appear. If there is already a useable Phonebook entry, you can go to Step 7 in this task. Though we already have a useable phone-book entry, we are going to choose the **New** button to start the wizard to add a phonebook entry.

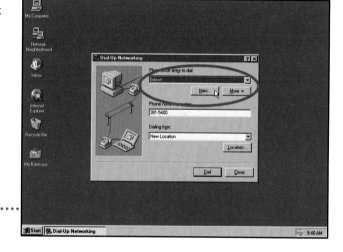

Puzzled?

A phonebook is a list of dial-up entries that you use to dial and access other networks.

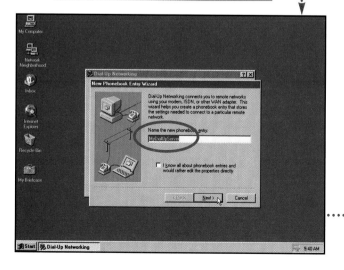

3 The **New Phonebook Entry Wizard** will appear. Provide a name for this phonebook entry, and press the **Next** button.

4 The next step in the wizard asks for information about the server that you are calling. When using an Internet service provider, checking the first option (by clicking once in the box **I am calling the Internet**) should be sufficient. For more information, call either the service provider or the administrator of the network being accessed. After checking the appropriate choices, press the **Next** button.

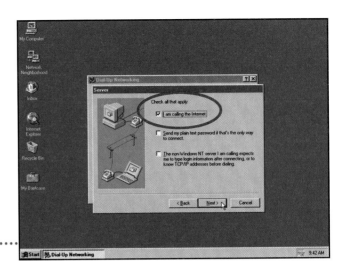

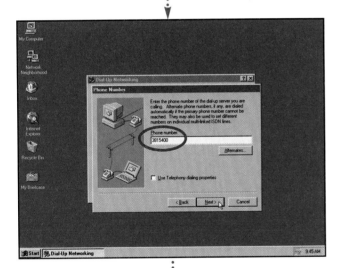

5 Next, the wizard asks for the phone number you are calling. If there is more than one number (secondary access number) that can be used, others can be added by pressing the **Alternates** button, and then by adding them. This provides an alternative in case you often get a busy signal or have other problems with the primary phone number. After adding the phone number or numbers, press the **Next** button.

6 The final wizard window appears. If there are any changes you wish to make before saving the entry, use the **Back** button to move to a section and make changes. When completed, press the **Finish** button to save the changes. The New Phonebook Entry Wizard will close.

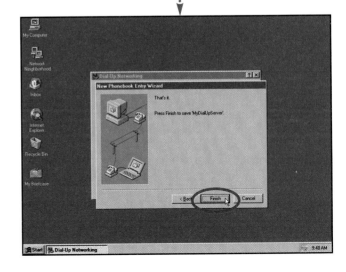

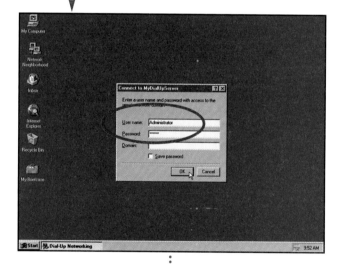

7 The **Dial-Up Networking** dialog box will open. Check that the proper **Phonebook entry to dial** is selected at the top of the dialog, and press the **Dial** button.

Missing Link

Windows NT has very advanced network capabilities. It will perform tasks to establish communications to a remote network. However, at times, it may be necessary to make certain changes to a Dial-Up Networking phonebook entry to establish a connection. If you are unable to establish a connection, contact your service provider or network administrator.

8 If this is the first time using this entry, you will be prompted for a **Username** and **Password**. Then choose the **OK** button.

Puzzled?

Dial-Up Networking may prompt you for a username and password. This may seem strange since Windows NT already has your username and password. However, this information may be different on the network that you are remotely connecting to. Therefore, NT allows you to provide a separate username and password for the remote network.

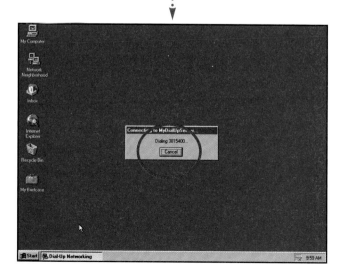

9 A message box will alert you to the status of your call. If connected successfully, Windows NT may now use the other network's resources. If not successfully connected, you may need to change one or more of the settings for the phonebook entry. The Dial-Up Networking Common Problems table deals with the most common problems. ■

Task 48: Dial-Up Networking

Dial-Up Networking Common Problems

Problem	Solution
By default, Windows NT does not use a login script for phonebook entries. This is the most common cause of unsuccessful attempts to connect to a remote network.	To change this setting, press the **More** button in the Dial-Up Networking dialog and choose the **Edit Entry and Modem Properties** command. Another dialog appears with several tabs. Choose the **Script** page by clicking its tab. Choose the **Run this script** radio button and **Generic login** from the drop down list box immediately below the radio button. Press the **OK** button and try to dial again.
Many networks that provide remote connections with information about how to find resources on that network. However, some do not. If the network you are dialing does not, you will have to provide more information to be able to use resources on this network. in thePrimary DNS section, enter the numbers that	Open the **Edit Phonebook Entry** as described in step 9 and choose the server page. Check that the server type matches that of the network being dialed. Then, press the **TCP/IP Settings** button. In the TCP/IP Settings dialog box, choose the Specify **name server address radio** button. Then, your service provider or network administrator provides you with for this entry. Press **OK** for the two dialogs and choose the **Dial** command again. If problems continue, contact your service provider or network administrator.

E-Mail Accounts

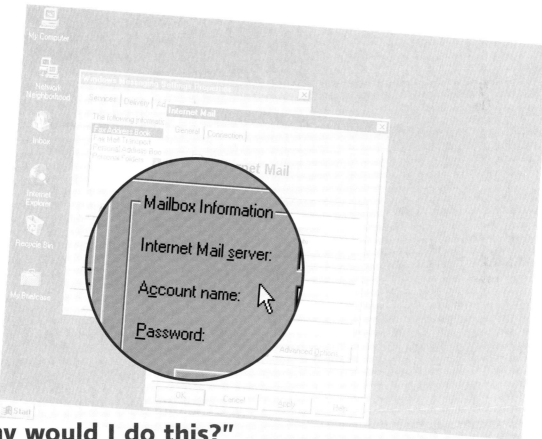

"Why would I do this?"

Electronic mail is a very powerful tool that allows text, sound, and video to be sent to others. These messages are sent using e-mail addresses. Accounts are used to administer the use of e-mail and addresses are used to identify users. To use the e-mail tools that interact with the Windows messaging system, you must provide information about your e-mail account using information provided by your Internet service provider or network administrator.

1 On the Windows NT desktop, there is an icon named **Inbox** that looks like a globe with a stack of letters next to it. Right-click this icon and choose the **Properties** command.

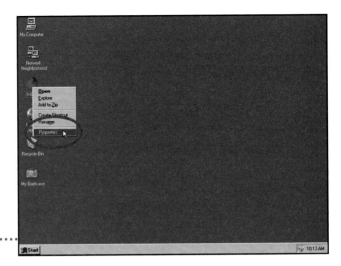

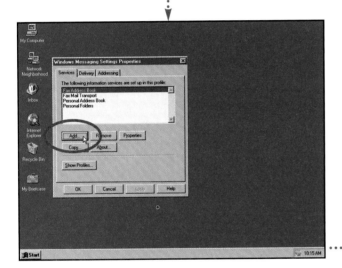

2 The **Windows Messaging Settings Properties** dialog box will appear. To add the Internet Mail service, press the **Add** button.

3 The **Add Service to Profile** dialog box will appear with a list of the installed services that can be added. Choose the **Internet Mail** service, and press the **OK** button.

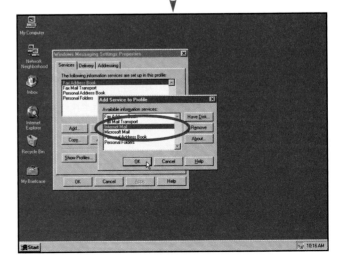

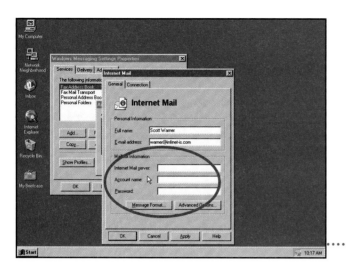

4 The **Internet Mail** dialog box will open. On the **General** page, enter your personal and mailbox information. Your Internet service provider or network administrator must provide you with an e-mail address and mailbox information.

5 Next, press the **Connection** tab to show the Connection page of the Internet Mail dialog box. Choose whether you will be using e-mail from a modem, a server on your network, or if you will have to connect to a remote network to access this e-mail account. If you are dialing a remote network, you *must* have a Dial-Up Networking phonebook entry for that system. If you would like to have mail retrieved on a regularly scheduled basis, press the **Schedule** button in the Transferring Internet Mail section.

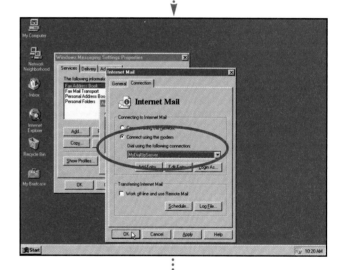

6 A **Schedule** dialog box appears and allows you to choose how often to check for messages. Choose **OK** in all of the dialog boxes to save your changes. ■

Puzzled?

If your computer keeps dialing the modem, establishing a connection, and disconnecting, you may have it set-up to check for e-mail on a remote network periodically. To change this setting, go to the Connection page of the Internet Mail dialog box.

Sending E-Mail

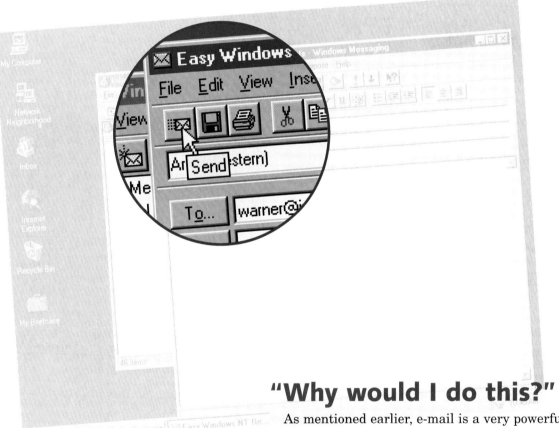

"Why would I do this?"

As mentioned earlier, e-mail is a very powerful tool. However, it must be used to realize this power. The windows messaging system provides several tools that when used in combination allow you to send e-mail to others.

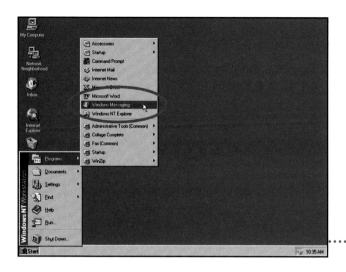

1 Open the **Start** menu and choose the **Programs** command. From the **Programs** menu choose the **Windows Messaging** command. Or, you could double-click the **Inbox** icon on the desktop.

2 The **Inbox** window appears. It displays your personal folders and any messages contained in the selected folder. To compose a new message, press the **New Message** button on the toolbar. Or you can select **New Messsage** from the **Compose** menu. A **New Message** window opens.

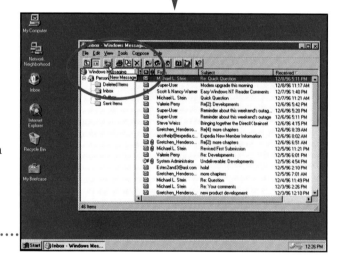

3 The **New Message** dialog box opens. In the **To...** edit box enter the address **warner@infinet-is.com (the authors' e-mail address**.) Next, enter **Easy Windows NT Reader Comments** in the **Subject** edit box. Finally enter any comments or questions you have about the book in the body of the message. When finished, press the **Send** button on the toolbar.

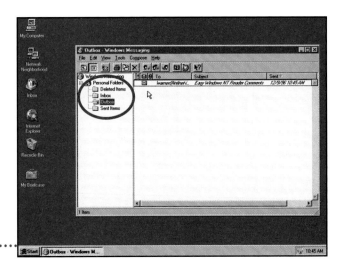

4 Now in the **Inbox** window, select the **Outbox** folder. You can see that the message is ready to be sent.

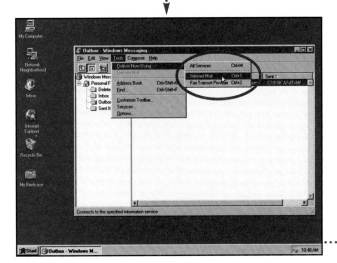

5 When you are ready to send the Internet Mail messages in the Outbox, choose the **Tools** menu. Selecting the **Deliver Now Using** command will to bring up a secondary menu. Choose the **Internet Mail** command.

6 Any Internet Mail messages in the Outbox folder will be sent. Now choose the **Sent Items** folder to see that the message was sent. ■

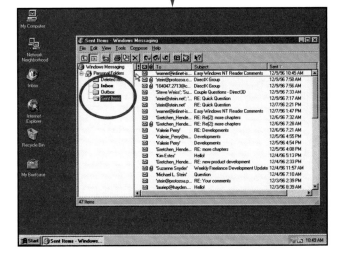

Receiving E-Mail

"Why would I do this?"

After you have sent e-mail, you will hopefully
receive responses. These responses can be
retrieved several ways using the tools of the
Windows messaging system.

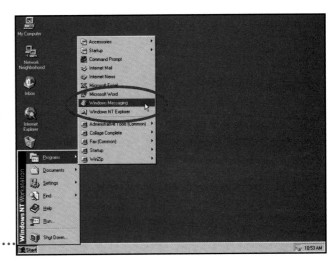

1 Open the **Start** menu and choose the **Programs** command. From the **Programs** menu choose the **Windows Messaging** command. Or, you could double-click the **Inbox** icon on the desktop.

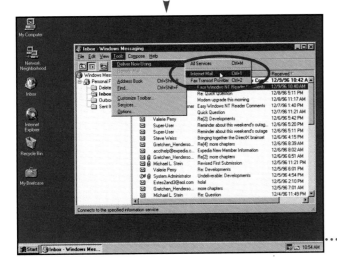

2 Open the **Tools** menu and select the **Deliver Now Using** command. Choose the **Internet Mail** command from the secondary menu.

3 If you have any new messages, the **Inbox** folder will be bolded. Click once on the **Inbox** folder, and you can see the e-mail header information. To read the message, double-click the header. ■

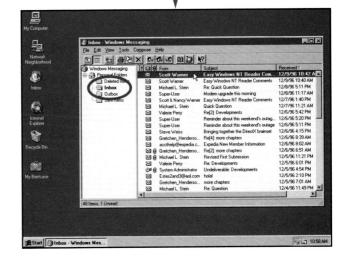

Browsing the World Wide Web

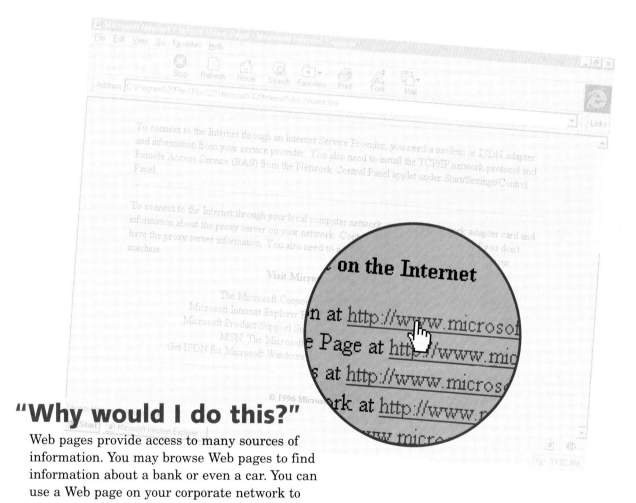

"Why would I do this?"

Web pages provide access to many sources of information. You may browse Web pages to find information about a bank or even a car. You can use a Web page on your corporate network to view accounting reports or sign up for health benefits.

1 A Web browser is used to view web pages. Windows NT comes with the **Microsoft Internet Explorer** Web browser. Double-click the desktop icon of a globe and magnifying glass, labeled **Internet Explorer**, to start the Web browser.

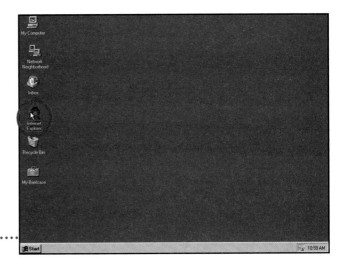

2 Initially, Internet Explorer will open to a Web page that Microsoft has supplied on your local machine. This page gives some brief explanations using a Web browser and some Microsoft Web pages that may be helpful.

Missing Link

By default, Internet Explorer opens a local Web page. This is called the home page. This page can be changed to any page that is reachable by your Web browser by choosing **Options** from the **View** menu.

3 If you do not have Internet access through your local network, use Dial-Up Networking to connect to your Internet service provider. Scroll to the bottom of the page that is initially displayed in the Internet Explorer. With the mouse pointer, click the underlined and colored text **http://www.microsoft.com**. This is the Uniform Resource Locator address of a web page. URLs are used to allow web pages to reside on any type of computer. An URL can be indicated by underlined and colored text or can be embedded in a picture.

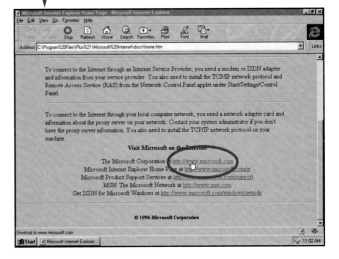

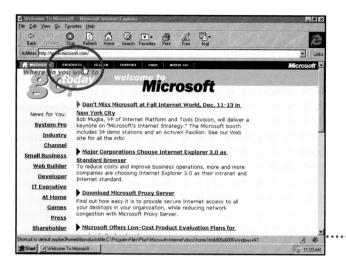

4 Now, your Web browser will be displaying a Microsoft Web page that is located on a Microsoft server on a remote network. You can navigate this site by clicking other URLs or graphics which contain URLs. Click the word **PRODUCTS** at the top of the page to view a list of Microsoft products.

Puzzled?

The Microsoft Web pages displayed in your Web browser will most likely be different from the ones shown in this book. That is because Microsoft updates these pages often to keep their information current.

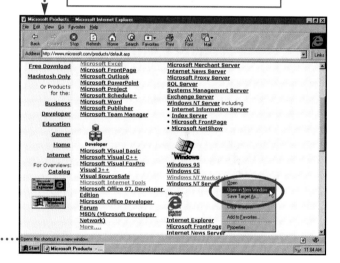

5 The Web browser opens a page displaying URLs or links to pages with information about specific Microsoft products. To view the product information page in a separate window while keeping the list page open, right click the product you wish to view **(Windows NT Workstation)** and choose the **Open in New Window** command from the quick menu.

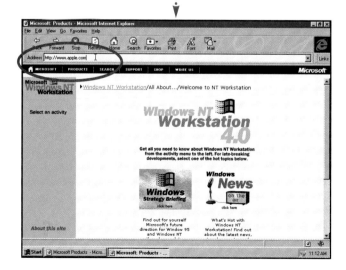

6 After viewing this page, you remember viewing a page about a competing product and want to quickly check that page for comparison. If you know the URL, you can simply type it into the **Address** edit box at the top of the page viewing area and press the **Enter** key on your keyboard. ■

Downloading Files from the Internet

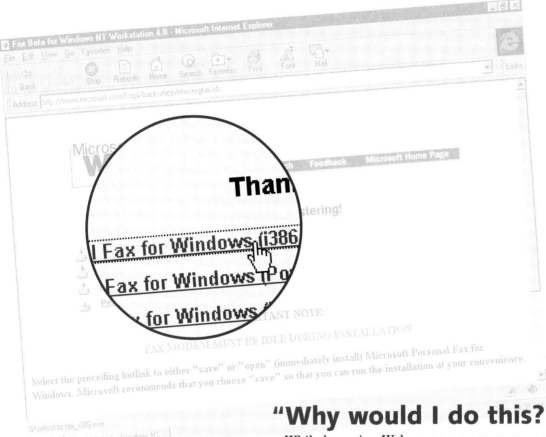

"Why would I do this?"

While browsing Web pages, you may come across a service that you are interested in. This service may allow you to download an application to fill out and mail back. Or, you may need a piece of software necessary to complete a task or allow a piece of hardware to function properly. There are many reasons why you may need to download a file from the Internet.

166

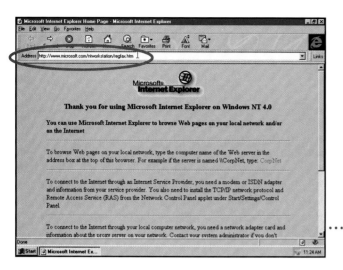

1 Start your Web browser (refer to Task 52), enter the URL **http://www.microsoft. com/ntworkstation/regfax.htm**, and press the **Enter** key on your keyboard.

Puzzled?

You may experience strange behavior from beta software. This is due to its experimental nature. Companies distribute the software, so users can identify problems that the company may not want to produce. If you have problems while using beta software, be sure to report it to the software supplier.

2 Fill out the requested information on the Web page and press the **Register** button at the bottom of the page.

Missing Link

If you are not able to answer some of the registration questions, press the spacebar a couple times to enter a blank. Some registration forms will not allow you to leave any information blank. Or, sometimes you do not want to supply personal information.

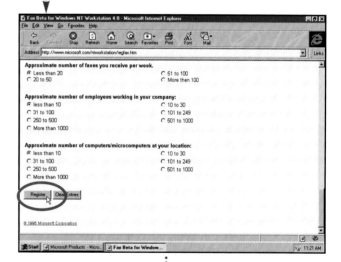

3 Click the **Personal Fax** for Windows link that matches your hardware configuration. We are going to choose **Personal Fax for Windows (i386 – 611KB)**.

4 Internet Explorer will prompt you to either run the file or save it to a disk. Choose the **Save it to disk** radio button and press the **OK** button.

Missing Link

Files available for downloading could contain computer viruses. To avoid encountering such a file, use an anti-virus program or only download files that you know are secure and free of viruses.

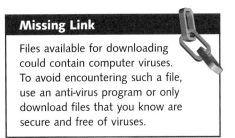

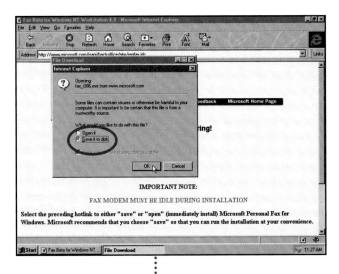

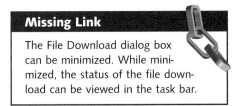

5 The Save As dialog will prompt you for the location and file name to use for saving this file. Enter the appropriate information and press the **Save** button.

Missing Link

The File Download dialog box can be minimized. While minimized, the status of the file download can be viewed in the task bar.

6 Internet Explorer will display a status dialog box that displays the progress of the file download. The download can be canceled at any time by pressing the **Cancel** button in the **File Download** dialog box. ■

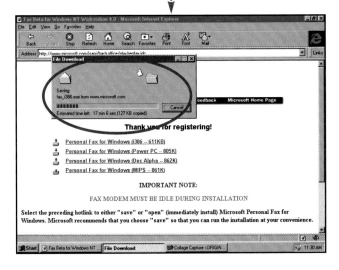

PART VIII

Using Windows NT Accessories

WINDOWS NT PROVIDES many applications that you can use to help you with your work, to be creative, or to have fun. These accessory applications are not as powerful as larger applications that you purchase and install on Windows NT, but they are useful for specific purposes. If you open your Accessories menu off the **Start**, **Programs** menus, you will see all the different options you have available. We are only going to cover a few of the most common accessories.

Paint allows you to create, edit, and save screen captures, clip art, and drawings. Paint is a great application if you need to view or make modifications to saved artwork.

Windows NT also provides multimedia tools, such as the CD Player, so you can play music CDs or the Media Player to view film and audio clips. You can record sounds, play them back, and incorporate them into presentations.

If you have not yet purchased a word processing application, you will find that WordPad is quite capable. It is a limited version of the Microsoft Word word processor and can be used to view or edit Word files. While in WordPad, you can change fonts, increase or decrease type sizes, set and remove tabs, and alter text alignment to the left, right, or center. You can even create bulleted lists, insert objects like a paint file, or paste text from other applications.

The option to send faxes directly from your computer is another great feature of Windows NT. When you have your modem set up correctly, you can fax documents as easily as you print them. Microsoft Personal Fax is simple to use: You set up your fax option, and follow the Fax Wizard instructions, and off it goes.

Just when you think "it's all work and no play," Windows NT lets you "play," too. There are several games provided for you. These games can help break the tension of the day and improve your ability to maneuver the mouse.

Windows NT makes it possible to cut, copy, and paste information between applications. If you wanted to copy a portion of a memo and paste it into your fax coversheet, this can be done easily. In the Windows NT background, you are actually using an application called the Clipboard Viewer.

The Windows NT Accessories are programs that help you use your computer. Though you can purchase more powerful versions of the accessories, the ones supplied with Windows NT are sufficient for most new users.

TASK

Using Paint

"Why would I do this?"

You can use Paint to create drawings, images, diagrams, or any kind of art you want. You can also use Paint to edit graphics like clip art, scanned art, or graphic files from other applications. You can add free-form lines, shapes, airbrush paint, brush strokes, text, and more. Along with all the things you can add and create, you can alter the way they look by flipping, rotating, and inverting color.

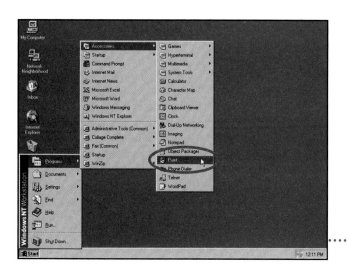

1 Open the **Start** menu and choose the **Programs** command. From the **Programs** menu, select the **Accessories** folder. From the **Accessories** menu, choose the **Paint** command.

2 The **Paint** window opens with a blank work area and the **Pencil** tool active. Drag the pencil tool around while pressing the left mouse button to get the feel for free-hand drawing.

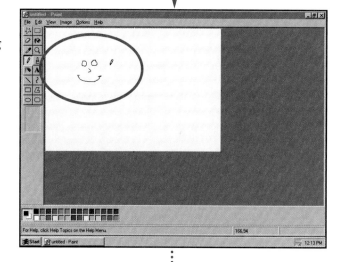

Missing Link

If you ever do not like what you have drawn, you can open the **Edit** menu and choose **Undo**. You can Undo a total of three tasks; each time you make a change to your work area. You must select **Edit Undo** for each task you want to undo.

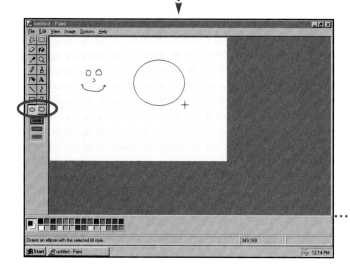

3 On the toolbar, click the **Circle** tool and draw a circle in the work area. Click the left mouse button on the pointer tool and drag it diagonally down and to the right to create the shape.

4 Click the **Paint Can** tool from the toolbar. Now select a color from the color palette by clicking once with the left mouse button on a color. Place the Paint pointer somewhere inside the circle and click once.

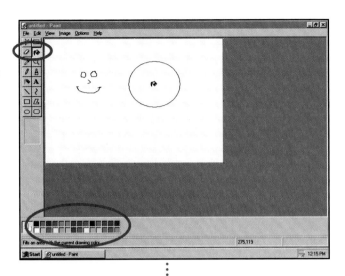

Missing Link

You can create a new color for your color palette by double-clicking any of the colors. The Edit Colors dialog box appears. By choosing the **Define Custom Colors** button, you can create any color you like; then choose the **Add to Custom Colors** button.

5 The circle will fill with the color you selected. Now choose the **Select** tool from the toolbar.

6 Click the work area and drag the dotted rectangle so that it outlines the freehand drawing.

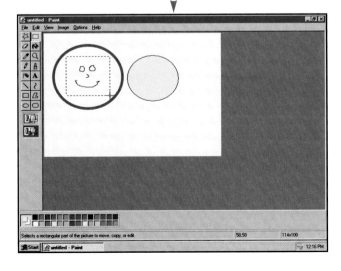

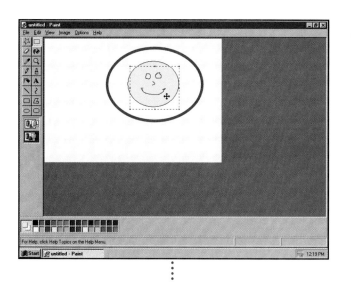

7 Place the pointer inside the boxed area. Notice the pointer has turned into a cross arrow. Now you can click somewhere directly inside the dashed line box area and drag to another location. The dashed lines disappear. When you have moved the selected area to where you want, release the mouse button (notice the dashed lines appear again), and click somewhere outside the selected area. This is how you can move objects in your graphics.

8 Now open the **View** menu and choose the **Zoom** command. A secondary menu appears. Select **Custom**.

Missing Link

While you have a section of your work selected, you could press the **Delete** key to delete the selected area; or open the **Image** menu and choose the **Flip/Rotate** command to rotate your selected area.

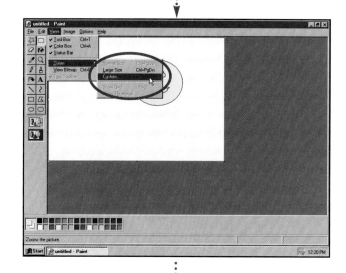

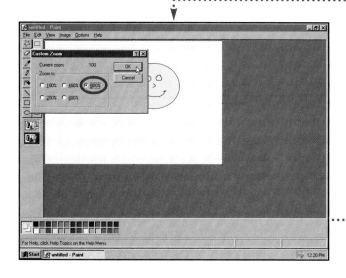

9 From the Custom Zoom dialog box that appears, choose the **800%** radio button and then the **OK** button.

10 The work area is magnified 800 times, and the visible area covers a smaller space. You are now able to alter your image, one pixel at a time. On the tool-bar, click the **Pencil** command. In the color palette, there are two squares, one on top of the other. The top-left box is the color associated with the left mouse button. The bottom-right box is the color associated with the right mouse button. Choose the colors you want to use to edit your work, and make any changes you want.

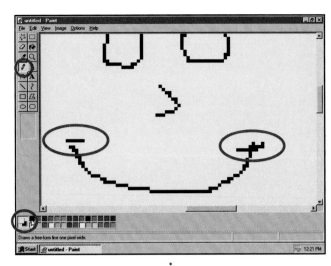

11 When you are finished, open the **View** menu and choose the **Zoom, Normal Size** command.

Puzzled?

Notice that after editing the pixels on the smiley face, the smile is more even and the right eye is more of a circle.

12 Now you can see the changes that you have made. If you want to save your work, open the **File** menu and choose the **Save** command (see Task 28, "Saving Your Work"); otherwise, choose the **Close (X)** button. ■

Missing Link

To open and edit this or any other image in Paint, open the **File** menu and choose the **Open** command. You can select a file you want to edit by double-clicking the file. Then edit the file, save your work, and close the application.

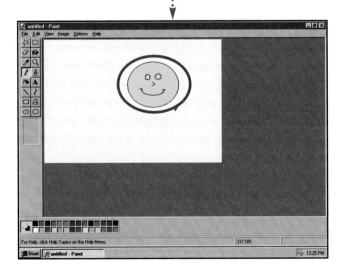

Controlling Multimedia

"Why would I do this?"

You can use the CD Player in Windows NT to listen to music while you work, depending on your computer's configuration and your office policy. You can use the Volume Control to regulate the volume. Many people download movie clips from the Internet and watch them using the Media Player. You can also add new and fun sounds to your computer with the Sound Recorder, as long as you have a microphone. All of these multimedia options require a sound card, an adapter that has digital sound reproduction capabilities.

Task 55: Controlling Multimedia

1 Open the **Start** menu and choose the **Programs** command. From the **Programs** menu, select the **Accessories** folder. From the **Accessories** menu, choose the **Multimedia** command. You now have four different multimedia controls to choose from.

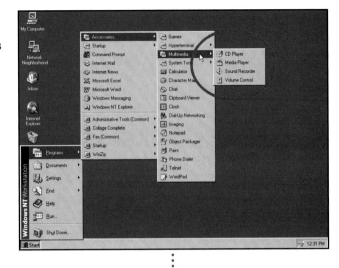

Missing Link

To use the Sound Recorder, you must have a sound card and speakers installed on your computer. If you want to record live sound, you also need a microphone.

2 Choose the **CD Player** to play audio compact discs from a CD-ROM. When you put a CD into the drive and close it, Windows NT should start playing the CD automatically.

Missing Link

If you have a sound card, you can use the Volume Control when you play audio files. You can select the **Volume Control** from the **Start** menu or from the CD Player (or from the speaker on the system tray), open the **View** menu and choose **Volume Control**.

3 Choose the **Media Player** to play audio, video, or animation files, and to control the settings for multimedia hardware devices. To use the Media Player, you should also have a sound card. However, you can view video without a sound card. To close the multimedia devices, click the **Close (X)** button. ∎

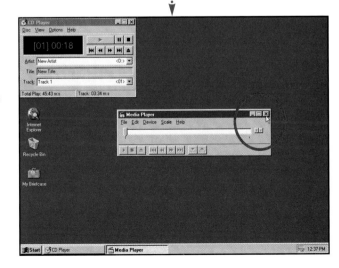

Writing and Editing in WordPad

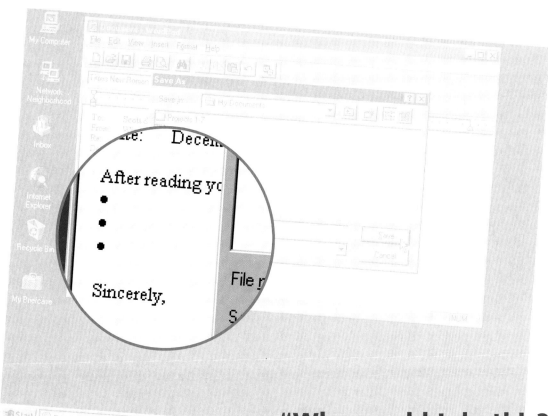

"Why would I do this?"

You can use WordPad to edit text files or create quick documents such as notes or fax sheets. WordPad allows you to save files in four different formats: Word for Windows (default), a rich-text document with formatting, a text document without any formatting, or a DOS format.

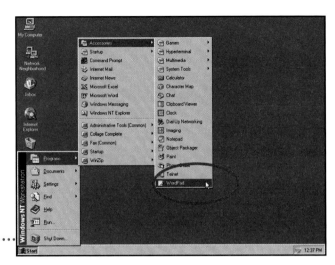

1 Open the **Start** menu and choose the **Programs** command. From the **Programs** menu, select the **Accessories** folder. From the **Accessories** menu, choose the **WordPad** command.

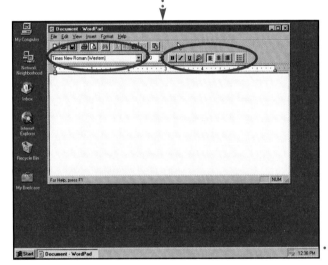

2 The **WordPad** window appears with a blank area for writing and editing text. Familiarize yourself with the menus and toolbar by clicking the menus and seeing the options you have. Notice that the main toolbar and menus are very similar to Microsoft Word.

3 Type the following information. **To:**, press the **<Tab>** key, **Scott & Nancy Warner**, and press the **Enter** key. **From:**, **<Tab>**, (**Your Name**), and **Enter**. **Re:**, **<Tab>**, **Easy Win NT**, and **Enter**. And finally, **Date:**, **<Tab>**, and from the **Insert** menu, choose the **Date and Time** command.

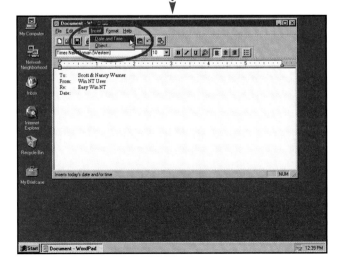

Missing Link

Pressing **Enter** creates a *hard return*, which is a new paragraph. The cursor will be blinking on the next line. If you make a mistake while typing, press the **Backspace** key to delete one character at a time.

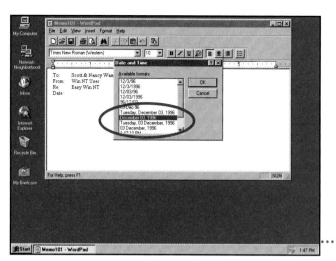

4 The Date and Time dialog box appears. Choose the format you want in your document, then choose the **OK** button. Today's date and/or time are automatically inserted into your document.

5 Press the **Enter** key twice, type in the sentence **After reading your book, I have the following comments:**, and press **Enter**. Press the **Enter** key once, then type the following information: **Sincerely**, press the **Enter** key three times, **(Your Name)**, and press the **Enter** key.

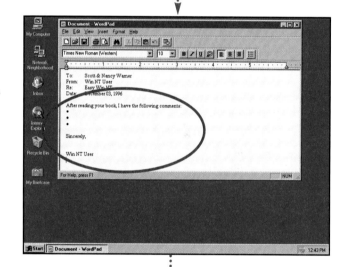

Missing Link

There are other options on the Format Bar (from left to right): Font and Font Size drop down list boxes; Bold, Italic, Underline, and Color buttons; Align Left, Center, Align Right. You can also find these options on the Format menu.

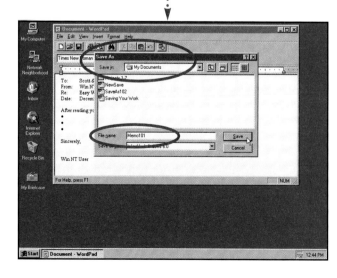

6 Save the file as **Memo101** by opening the **File** menu and choosing **Save**. The **Save As** dialog box appears. In the **Save In** list box, choose the **My Documents** folder and choose the **Save** button to save the document. You can close WordPad by choosing the **Close (X)** button. ■

TASK 57

Installing Fax Software

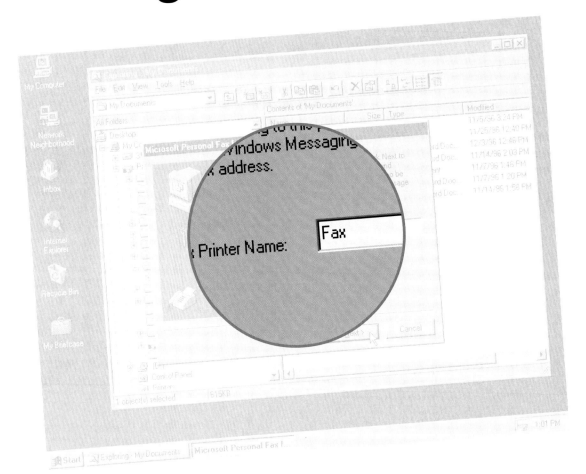

"Why would I do this?"

A feature of Windows 95 that does not come standard on Windows NT is the faxing software. However, Microsoft makes the software available for free on their World Wide Web site. In a previous task, you downloaded the fax software. In this task, you are going to install it. The following task shows you how to use the software.

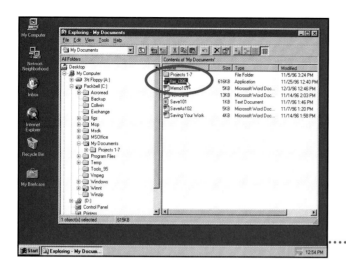

1 You must have a properly installed modem connected to your computer, an active phone line, and Microsoft Personal Fax installed on your computer. Open Windows NT Explorer from the **Start**, **Programs** menu. Locate the file you downloaded from the World Wide Web. Double-click the file **fax_i386.exe**; this launches the installation program.

2 A Microsoft Personal Fax message dialog box appears, telling you that it is extracting the files needed to use the faxing software.

Missing Link

Many software applications are large and take up a lot of disk space. In order to easily transfer them, they need to be compressed or *zipped*. Files that are extracted are being *decompressed*, or made larger again.

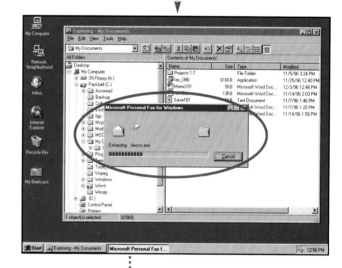

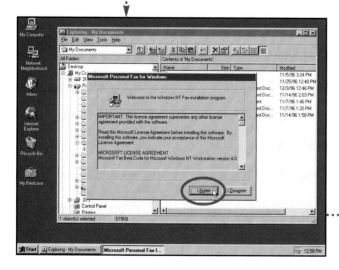

3 The Microsoft Personal Fax for Windows Wizard dialog box appears. This dialog box contains information about the Microsoft License Agreement, with which you can either agree or disagree. If you disagree and choose the **I Disagree** button, you cannot install the application and the wizard will cancel. If you agree and choose the **I Agree** button, the application continues.

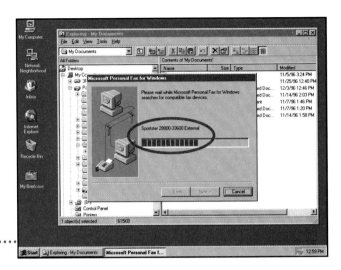

4 Microsoft Personal Fax for Windows searches for a fax modem installed on your computer. If it does not find one, you need to make sure you installed your modem correctly (or that it is indeed a modem that allows you to fax).

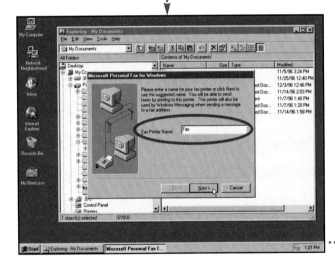

5 Microsoft Personal Fax for Windows asks that you enter a **Fax Printer Name**. This becomes one of your printer profiles. Choose the **Next** button.

6 The next wizard dialog box asks you for the telephone number that the fax modem will be using. Supply the requested information and choose the **Next** button.

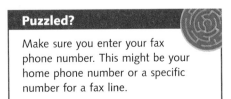

Puzzled?

Make sure you enter your fax phone number. This might be your home phone number or a specific number for a fax line.

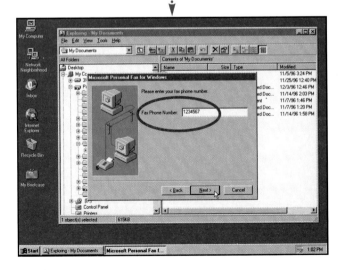

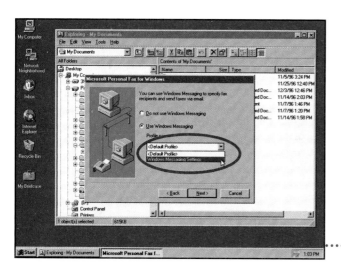

7 At the next wizard dialog box, choose whether you want to use Windows Messaging. Choose the **Use Windows Messaging** radio button and from the drop-down list box, choose **Windows Messaging Settings**. Choose the **Next** button.

8 At the next wizard dialog box, you need to choose the location that you want incoming faxes to be automatically stored. Choose the default unless you have a specific location you would like to use. Choose the **Next** button.

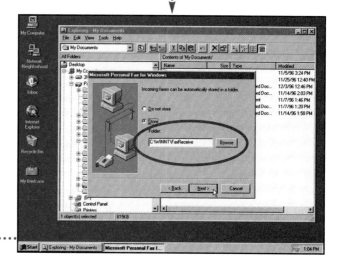

9 At the next wizard dialog box, you need to choose whether you want incoming faxes to be automatically printed. If you want them to be printed automatically, choose the **Print** radio button and the printer of your choice from the drop-down list box. Choose the **Next** button.

10 In a Windows Messaging personal folder, you need to choose whether you want incoming faxes to be automatically stored. If you want them to be stored automatically, choose the **Store** radio button and the profile name **Windows Messaging Setting** from the drop-down list box. Choose the **Next** button.

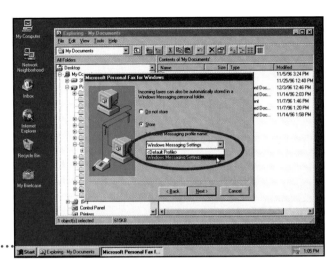

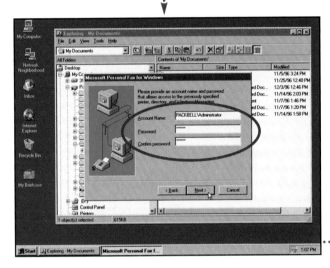

11 The next wizard wants you to provide a user account name. Use the account name and password that you set up or your Administrator gave you. This will probably be the default. Make sure you type your password and confirm it. Choose the **Next** button.

12 You are then asked to wait while Microsoft Personal Fax for Windows copies the appropriate files to your hard disk. You are now ready to send and receive faxes. Choose the **Finish** button. ∎

Missing Link

A final message dialog box might appear, asking you whether you want to restart the computer to let the settings activate. Close any of the applications you have open and choose the **Yes** button.

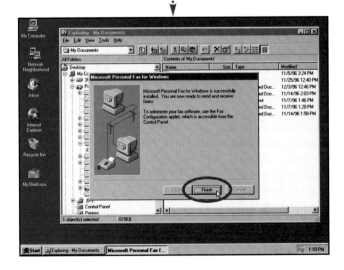

Using Microsoft Personal Fax for Windows NT

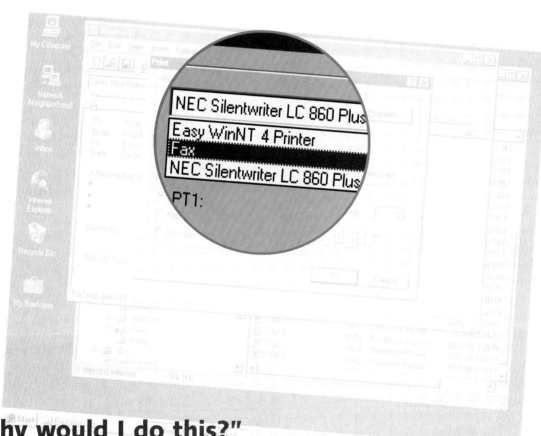

"Why would I do this?"

You can use Microsoft Personal Fax to send and receive faxed messages. You can view and print the faxes as well as send them from a print-enabled application in which you create them (by choosing File, Print) in Word or WordPad, for example. This task shows you how to send a fax using the Fax Wizard.

Task 58: Using Microsoft Personal Fax for Windows NT

1 There are a few ways to fax documents within Windows NT. The first way is from directly within a document. Let's use Memo101 from the previous task, within WordPad. If WordPad is not still open, start the application from the **Start**, **Programs**, **Accessories** menu. On the **File menu,** the **Memo101** document should be one of the last documents you worked on. Otherwise, select **File**, **Open** and locate the **Memo101** document.

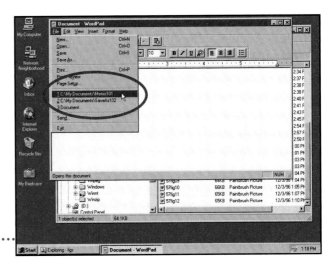

2 From the **File** menu, choose the **Print** command. The Print dialog box appears. Click once on the down arrow to the right of the **Printer Name** and choose the **Fax** profile. Choose the **OK** button.

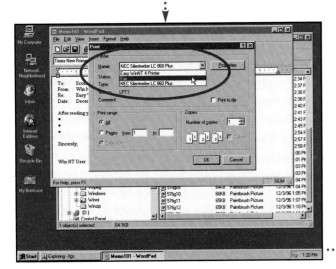

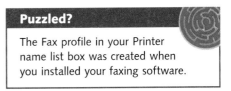

Puzzled?

The Fax profile in your Printer name list box was created when you installed your faxing software.

3 A Compose New Fax Wizard appears. Complete the information on who the fax is going to and what the telephone number is. Notice that you can send to multiple recipients by choosing the **Add** button. Choose the **Next** button.

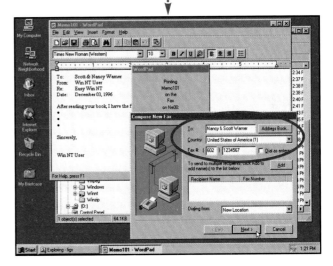

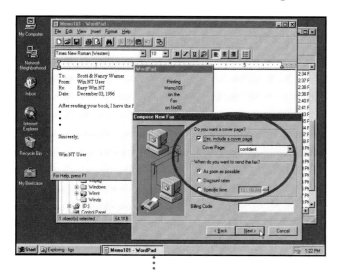

4 Select whether you want a cover page to be included and when you want the fax to be sent. Choose the **Next** button.

Missing Link

If you do not enter specific profile information that Windows NT needs to send the fax, a message box appears telling you what information you need to fill out. Fill in the additional information needed and choose the **OK** button.

5 Fill in the **Subject of Your Fax** and any **Additional Note** information. Choose the **Next** button.

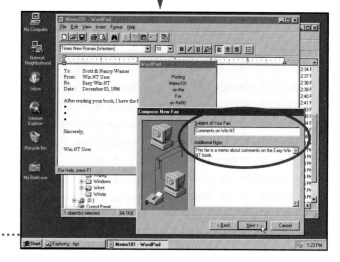

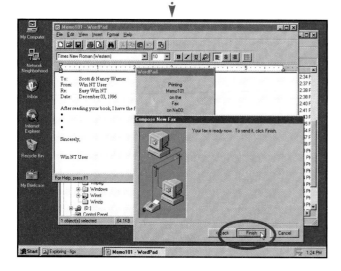

6 The last wizard appears, telling you that your fax is ready. You can choose the **Back** button to edit any of your choices. Choose the **Cancel** button if you do not want to send the fax. Or, choose the **Finish** button to send the fax. ■

Playing Games

"Why would I do this?"

Just because you use Windows NT to get your work done doesn't mean you can't have fun, too. Windows NT provides several games you can play to help break the tension of the day. Games also help improve your ability to maneuver the mouse.

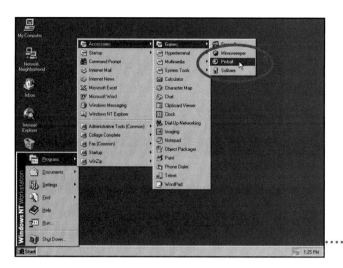

1 Open the **Start** menu and choose the **Programs** command. From the **Programs** menu, select the **Accessories** folder. From the **Accessories** menu, choose the **Games** folder. From the **Games** menu, choose the game you want to start. There are four games to choose from in Windows NT: FreeCell, Minesweeper, Pinball, and Solitaire. We are going to choose **Pinball** for this example.

2 The **3D Pinball** game opens up. If you need help playing the game, choose the **Help** menu and **Help Topics** for more information.

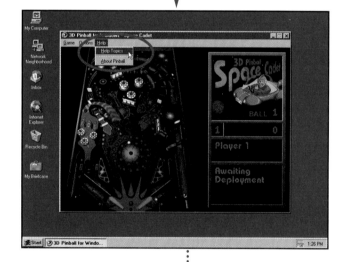

Missing Link

The objective of FreeCell is to move all the cards to the home cells, using the free cells as place-holders. In Minesweeper, you find all the mines on the field as quickly as possible without uncovering any of them. The objective of 3D Pinball is to launch the ball, and then get points by hitting bumpers, targets, and flags.

3 For information on the keyboard assignments for the game, choose the F8 key. You can use the assigned Player Controls or assign new ones. When you have assigned the controls, choose the **OK** button. If you ever want to set the Pinball Player Controls back to the default, choose the **Default** button. To close any game in Windows NT, click the **Close** button **(X)** in the title bar. ■

TASK 60

Using the Clipboard Viewer

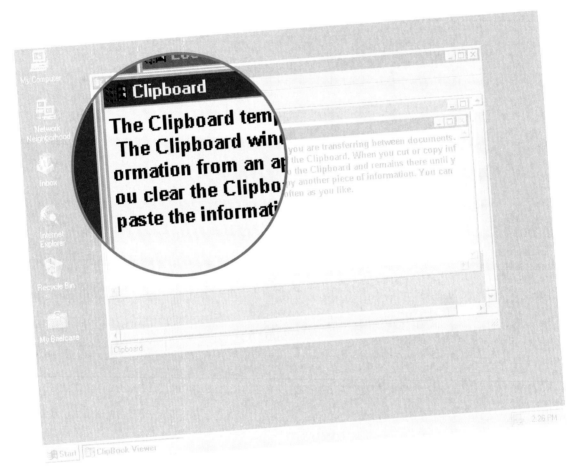

"Why would I do this?"

Windows NT makes it possible to cut, copy, and paste information between applications. In the Windows NT background, you are actually using an application called the Clipboard Viewer. The ClipBook Viewer window contains two smaller windows: the Local ClipBook and the Clipboard.

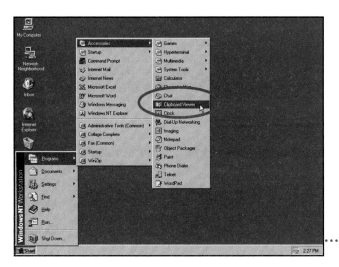

1 Open the **Start** menu and choose the **Programs** command. From the **Programs** menu, select the **Accessories** folder. From the **Accessories** menu, choose the **Clipboard Viewer** command.

2 The Clipboard and Local ClipBook windows open when you first start ClipBook Viewer. The ClipBook permanently stores information you want to save and shares with others. You can permanently save the contents of the Clipboard by copying it onto your Local ClipBook.

> **Missing Link**
>
> You can save several pieces of information (called pages) on the Local ClipBook and then copy the information back onto the Clipboard when you want to paste it into a document.

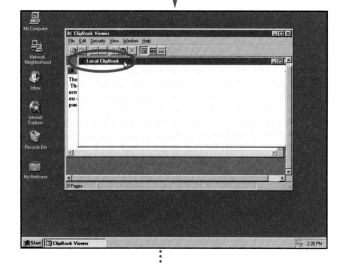

3 The Clipboard temporarily stores information you are transferring between documents. The Clipboard window shows the contents of the Clipboard. When you cut or copy information from an application, it is placed onto the Clipboard and remains there until you clear the Clipboard, or until you cut or copy another piece of information. You can paste the information into any document as often as you like. ■

PART IX

Windows NT Administrative Tools

WINDOWS NT WORKSTATION is a very powerful tool. Like most powerful tools, there is an inherent complexity that requires attention for proper function. There are a number of administrative tools supplied with Windows NT Workstation to help accomplish such maintenance tasks.

Users of the workstation must be maintained so that only authorized individuals may log on and take advantage of the workstation's resources. Hard drives must be maintained. Files must be backed up. They also must be protected from unauthorized viewing or manipulation. While all of this is happening, performance should be monitored.

TASK

61

Managing Users

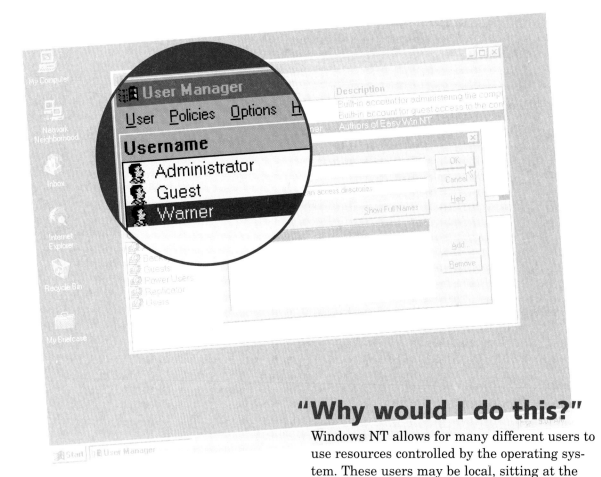

"Why would I do this?"

Windows NT allows for many different users to use resources controlled by the operating system. These users may be local, sitting at the computer, or accessing its resources over a network. Regardless of the method, these users must have an account on the NT machine being accessed.

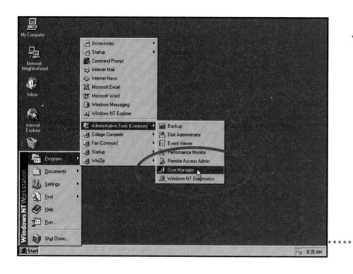

1 Open the **Start** menu and choose the **Programs** command. From the Programs menu, select the **Administrative Tools** folder. From the **Administrative Tools** menu, choose **User Manager**.

Missing Link

Windows NT sets up user groups that are granted specific types of privileges. New groups can be created, but cannot have the same privileges.

2 The **User Manager** window opens. There will be two sections. An upper section displays the user accounts for the workstation and the lower lists the groups that users may belong to. There are several groups set up by default.

Missing Link

Users do not need an account set up specifically for them to access resources shared to *Everyone*. For more information on sharing resources, see Task 43.

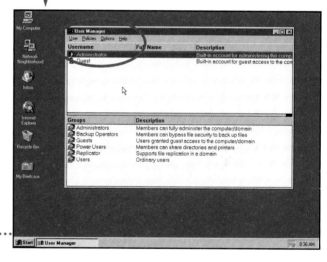

3 From the **User** menu, select the **New User** command.

Missing Link

Notice that we assigned a single username for two people. This is because multiple people need the same level of access to specific files. This has potential to be a security risk. If this is your computer at home, it's probably not a problem. If this is your computer at work, you would want to have separate usernames.

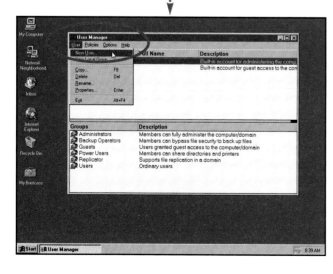

197

4 A **New User** dialog box will appear for entering information. **Username** and **Password** must be entered. There are also several check boxes to consider when creating a user. These are used to determine the longevity and security of the new user's password. Now choose the **Groups** button.

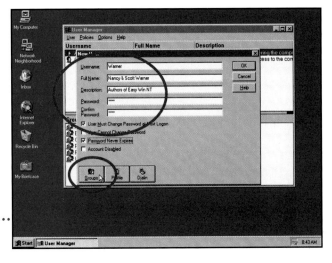

> ### Missing Link
>
> In addition to adding users in groups, you can also delete them by selecting the username or group in the **User Manager** dialog box, and choosing the **Delete** command from the **User** menu.

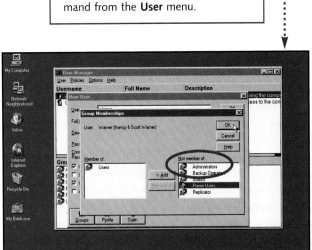

5 The **Groups** dialog box will appear. The pane on the left lists the groups that the new user belongs to. **Users** is listed by default. On the right, all available groups are listed. After choosing which groups the user will belong to, choose the **OK** button. Now go back to the **New User** dialog box to add the user. Choose the **OK** button, or choose **Cancel** to not add the user. If added, the user will now appear in the Username list.

6 Select the Username profile. From the **User** menu, select the **New Local Group** command. User accounts from this workstation can be members of the same local group. This allows users to access shared information, security, or whatever profile you establish for that group. In the dialog, enter the group name, a description, and which users will be members of this group. Choose **OK** to save the changes. The new group profile will appear in the lower section of the User Manager dialog box displaying groups. ■

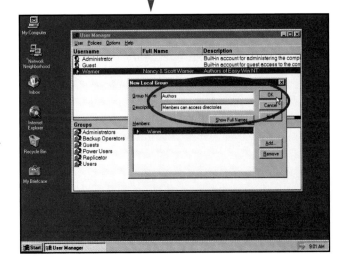

Monitor Hard Drives

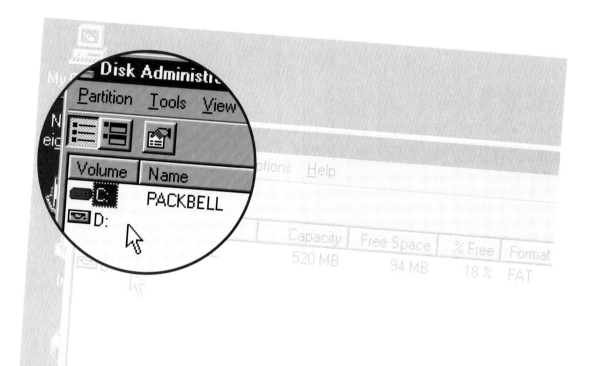

"Why would I do this?"

Windows NT workstations may have several disk drives. These drives may be physical, meaning that there are actually several hard disk drives connected to the machine. Or, they may be logical, meaning that a single hard disk drive has been partitioned into several disk drives. The Disk Administrator is a tool that can be used to view and modify these hard disk drives and any partitions they may contain.

Task 62: Monitor Hard Drives

1 Open the **Start** menu and choose the **Programs** command. From the Programs menu, select the **Administrative** Tools folder. From the **Administrative Tools** menu, choose the **Disk Administrator** command.

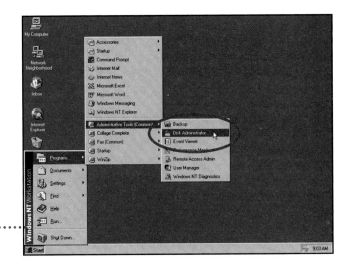

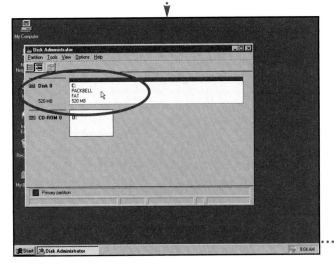

2 The **Disk Administrator** window appears showing the configuration of your workstation's disk drives. If this is the first time the Disk Administrator has been run, you will be prompted to acknowledge this fact and allow it to save your configuration.

3 To change the manner in which the information is being displayed, choose the **View Volumes** command from the **View** menu. Close the Disk Administrator by clicking the **Close (X)** button. ■

Puzzled?

The disk administrator may seem as if it doesn't do much. This can be the case on a machine with a single drive that has already been configured. But if you have several drives to configure and maintain, it is a single tool to accomplish these tasks from.

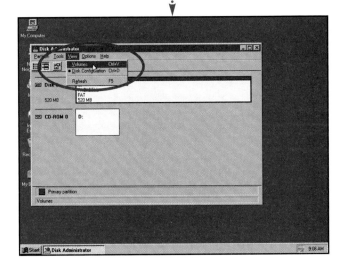

Backup Files

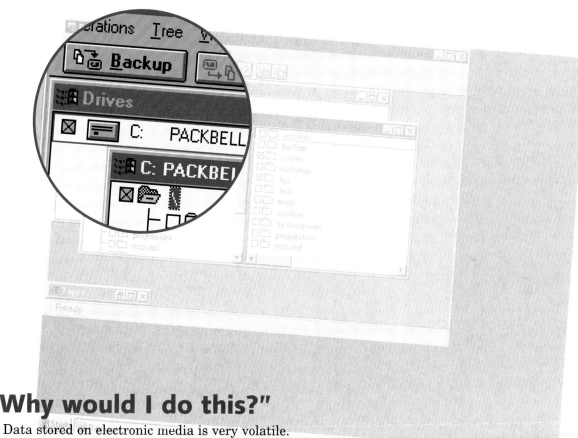

"Why would I do this?"

Data stored on electronic media is very volatile. It could be lost at any moment. To prevent the permanent loss of data, it can be backed up or copied to backup tape. This process can be done on a regular basis and the tapes can be stored at the same location or at a different location for added data security.

Task 63: Backup Files

1 Open the **Start** menu and choose the **Programs** command. From the **Programs** menu, select the **Administrative Tools** folder. From the **Administrative Tools** menu, choose the **Backup** command.

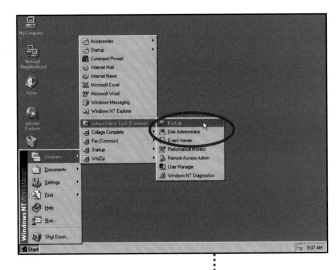

Missing Link

All drives, directories, and files with selected check boxes will be backed up. Selecting a directory also selects ALL of the directories and files inside of that directory. However, any directory or file can be deselected at any time.

2 The **Backup** window will appear with a **Drives** window and a **Tapes** window. The **Tapes** window will be minimized. To back up an entire disk drive, click the **Disk Drive** check box.

Puzzled?

If there is no tape drive properly installed on your machine, a message box will appear warning you of that fact and suggesting several possibilities why a tape drive may not function properly.

3 If you wish to back up only certain directories or files from a disk drive, double-click that disk drive. An additional window will appear that lists the disk's contents in a directory tree view (similar to Windows NT Explorer left column). Choose the directories and/or files that you wish backed up by clicking their check boxes. Place the backup tape in the tape drive and choose the **Backup** button. Enter the descriptive information and choose the **OK** button to proceed with the backup. ■

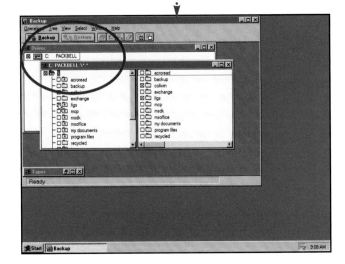

Monitor Performance

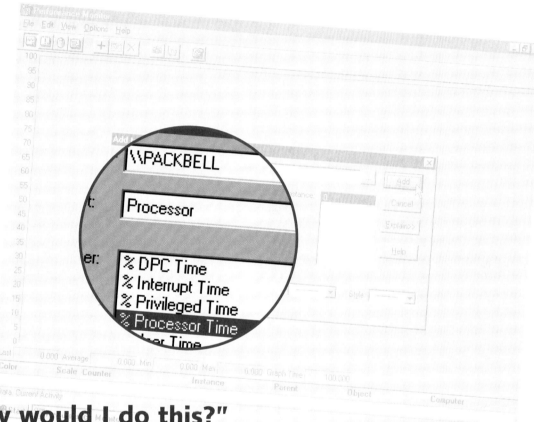

"Why would I do this?"

At times, you may notice that your workstation responds to your commands more slowly than others. Most likely this can be attributed to a process using an abundance of the available resources. The use of these resources can be monitored to determine which process is absorbing the majority of the workstation's resources. In addition, you can use this feature to monitor other machines over a network.

1 Open the **Start** menu and choose the **Programs** command. From the **Programs** menu, select the **Administrative Tools** folder. From the **Administrative Tools** menu, choose the **Performance Monitor** command.

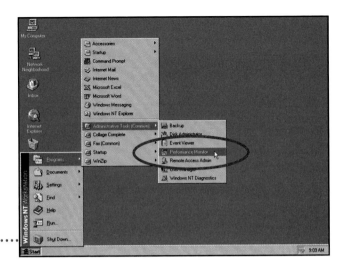

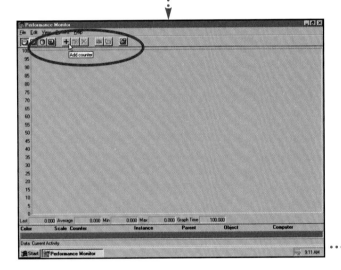

2 The **Performance Monitor** window opens, displaying a blank chart view. There are four methods of monitoring: chart, alert, log, and report. Chart, log, and report all display performance information in their own way. Alerts are used to alert the user when performance thresholds are broken. Choose the add button (**+**) in the toolbar.

3 An **Add to Chart** dialog appears, allowing you to add processes to the current view. The default will appear with the **Counter** set to **%Processor Time** and the **Object** set to **Processor**. Choose the **Add** button to add this counter to the current view. The counter will begin. To view the entire chart, choose the **Done** button.

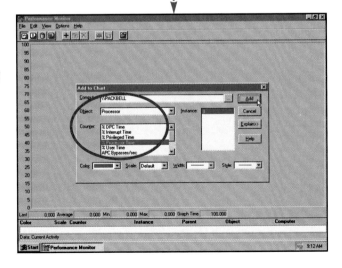

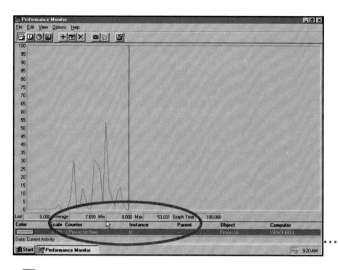

4 The bottom of the chart displays the processes being monitored, along with the color being used to display the information for each process. You can also view additional statistical information, such as minimum and maximum values.

5 To remove a counter on a chart, select the **Delete Selected Counter** button. You can also highlight it at the bottom of the chart and press the **Delete** key on the keyboard.

Missing Link

The Add to Chart Counter option has many processes that can be monitored. Many of the processes have similar names. At any time, you can choose the Explain button to receive a brief explanation of the current process in the Counter Explanation area at the bottom of the dialog box.

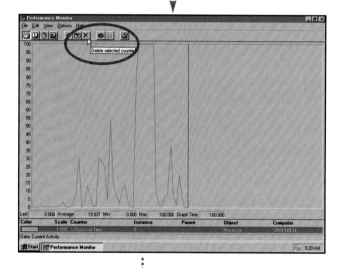

6 The chart is removed. Choose the **View the Alerts** button. Choose the add button **(+)** to enter the **Add to Alert** dialog box. If your hard disk has less than 10M free, you can set the Performance Monitor to alert you by running the WinZip utility. Choose **Logical Disk** in the **Object** drop down list box. Select **Free Megabytes** in the **Counter** list box and **0 ==> C:** in the **Instance** list box. Set **Alert If** to **Under 10** and **Run Program on Alert** to **C:\WINZIP\WINZIP** and **Every Time**. Skip that part. Choose **Add**. ■

Monitor Tasks

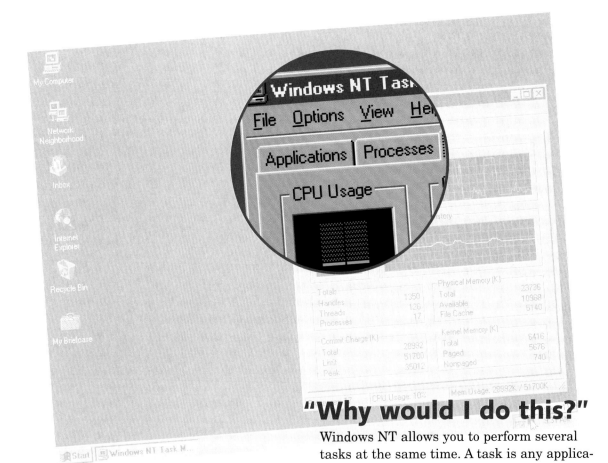

"Why would I do this?"

Windows NT allows you to perform several tasks at the same time. A task is any application, profile, or process that you access and utilize on your computer. To manage these tasks and the processes associated with them, Windows NT provides a Task Manager. In addition to its control functions, the Task Manager can also help you monitor performance.

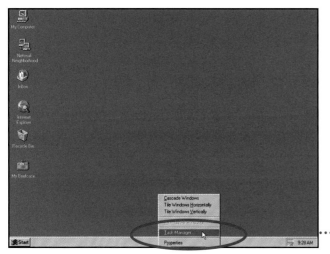

1 Right-click in any open spot on the task bar. A quick menu will appear, choose **Task Manager**.

Missing Link

To find the process associated with an application, right-click the application and choose **Go To Process**. The Processes page will be displayed and the application's process will be highlighted.

2 The **Windows NT Task Manager** dialog box appears. Click the **Applications** tab to view the applications currently running and their status. From this page, you can also end, switch to, or start a new task.

3 Click the **Processes** tab. Each process is displayed with statistical information. Individual processes can be ended by selecting them and choosing the **End Process** button. Use the End Process with caution. You could make your machine unstable.

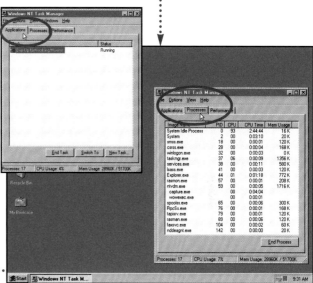

4 Click the **Performance** tab to view performance information. This page shows CPU and memory utilization. CPU and memory information can also be viewed from any of the pages in the status bar at the bottom of the Task Manager. ■

Puzzled?

If you do not find the CPU Usage History chart from the Performance page of the Task Manager very useful, you can minimize the Task Manager window. After doing this the current CPU Usage will be displayed in the system tray next to the clock.

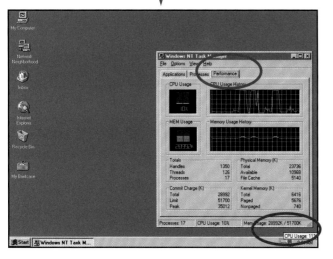

TASK 66

View Events

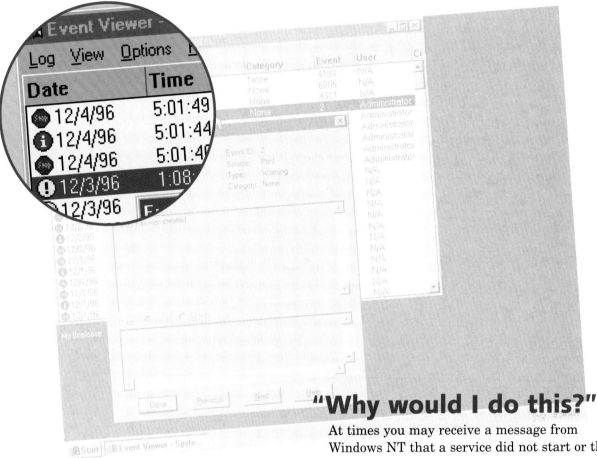

"Why would I do this?"

At times you may receive a message from Windows NT that a service did not start or that an error occurred. These messages are generated by events. A system event is an action, such as adding a new printer or fax capabilities, that generates a message. Records of these events are stored with detailed information about the event. You may view this information to determine the cause of the event.

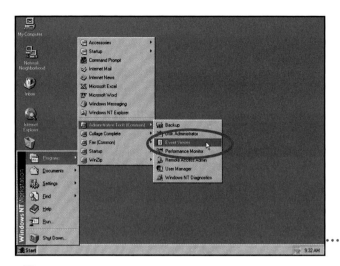

1 Open the **Start** menu and choose the **Programs** command. From the **Programs** menu, select the **Administrative Tools** folder. From the **Administrative Tools** menu, choose the **Event Viewer** command.

2 The **Event Viewer** appears displaying the Date, Time, and other information of all of the system events that have occurred. The icon that appears at the beginning of each event indicates the type of event it is.

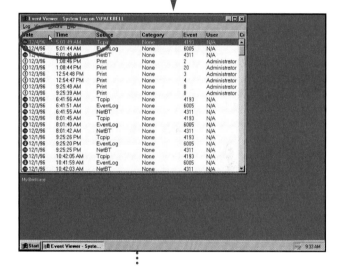

Puzzled?

The event log can become full. If this happens, you receive a message of that fact and you will have to empty the log. Before emptying the log, you can save it, or you could save and empty the log on a regular basis. Another option is to set it to automatically overwrite old entries with new ones when it reaches its maximum size.

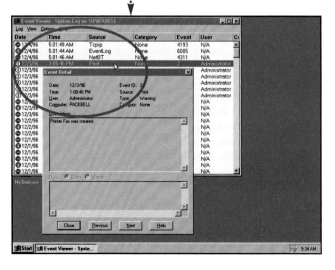

3 To view specific information for an event, simply double-click that event. An **Event Detail** dialog box will display more detailed information about the event. ■

Missing Link

There are also events generated for security and application events. These can be viewed by choosing their name (System, Security, Application) from the Log menu of the Event Viewer.

PART X

Personalizing Windows NT

THERE ARE MANY WAYS you can customize Windows NT. By customizing your desktop and other Windows NT features, you can make your work more enjoyable as well as efficient. You can adjust colors, settings, screen savers, and many other options to suit your own personal style. If you get tired of your changes, you can simply create new settings as many times as you like.

You use the Control Panel to modify many Windows NT settings, including the display, mouse, clock, keyboard, and more. Each setting that you can customize is represented by an icon in the Control Panel. These icons open to a dialog box that allows you to alter properties for that particular feature.

If you want your desktop to have some color, or you like a specific color *scheme* (group of colors), Windows NT has many desktop schemes from which you may choose. You can use patterns, wallpapers, or even load your own images. Alternatively, you can alter specific items like icon colors or desktop fonts.

Another feature that Windows NT lets you personalize, is the display settings. Depending on your video equipment (monitor, video card, adapter), Windows NT will help you to change your screen *resolution* (desktop area). This allows your screen to fit more items on your desktop. Additionally, you can change your screen colors to allow for more color variations.

Windows NT comes with many screen savers as well. Not only do they protect your monitor, but you can assign your screen saver to use your Windows NT password to restrict access to your session. Also, you can set your screen saver to come on when your computer has been idle for a specific time period.

If you are a new user, left-handed, or even a more advanced user, the ability to adjust your mouse is a great feature that Windows NT offers. You can alter the appearance of your mouse pointer and cursor.

Some people want the taskbar to appear all the time, while some want the taskbar only to be visible when they need it. You can personalize the taskbar so that it displays the clock, utilizes small or large icons on the Start menu, or always appears in the desktop foreground.

There are so many ways that Windows NT lets you customize your computer, that you are bound to find settings to fit you. This part shows you how to personalize Windows NT for a more comfortable environment.

Opening the Control Panel

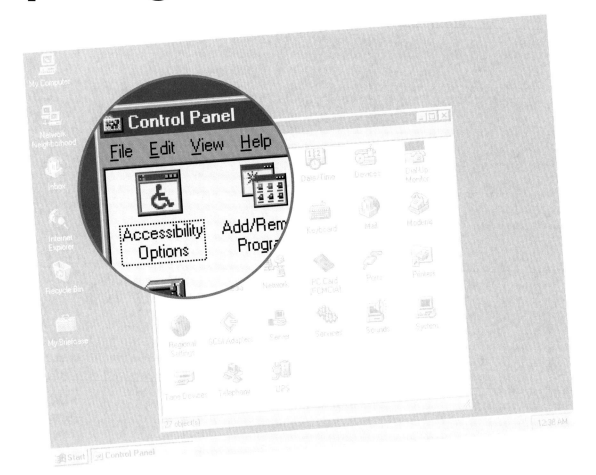

"Why would I do this?"

Windows NT has many settings that you can modify to change your environment. The way to change those settings is to open the Control Panel and select the item that you want to alter.

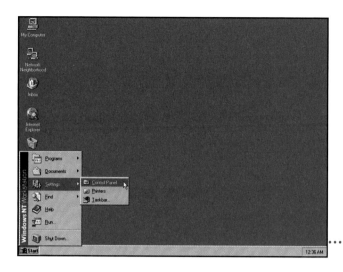

1 Open the **Start** menu and choose the **Settings** command. From the secondary menu, choose the **Control Panel** command.

2 The **Control panel** window opens. You can open any file in the Control Panel window by double-clicking the file's icon. You might need to enlarge your Control Panel window or scroll down to see all the icons available.

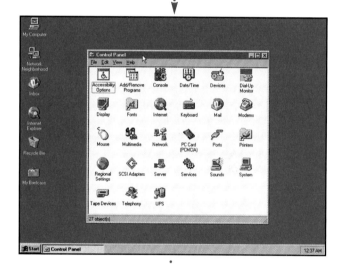

Missing Link

Many of the icons in the Control Panel window have been used throughout this book. If you want information on specific tasks for these icons, please refer to the index.

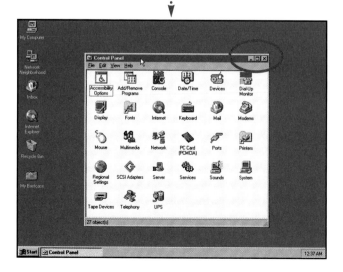

3 An alternative way to open the Control Panel is to double-click the **My Computer** icon, on your desktop. Then, double-click the **Control Panel** folder icon. The Control Panel window will open. ■

Missing Link

To close the Control Panel, click the **Close** button (**X**) in the title bar or simultaneously press the **Alt** and **F4** keys.

Changing the System Date and Time

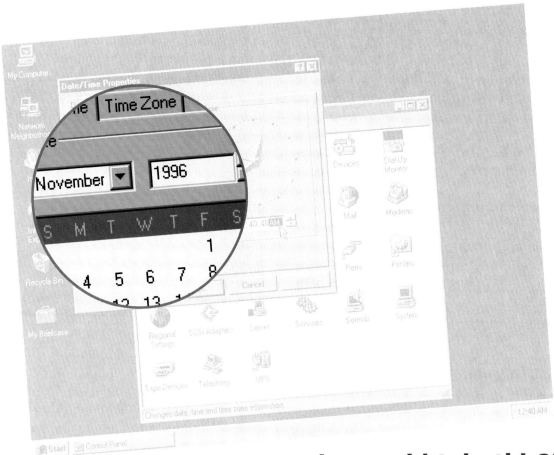

"Why would I do this?"

Your computer places a time and date stamp on every file you save. This is one way that you can identify a file for later use. In this task, we will learn how you can change your system's date, time, and time zone, in Windows NT.

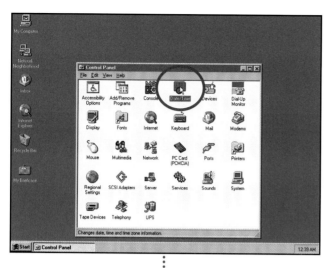

1 You should still have the **Control Panel** open. If not, from the **Start** menu, choose **Settings**, **Control Panel**. Double-click the **Date/Time** icon.

Missing Link

A faster way to display the Date/Time Properties dialog box is to double-click the time (??:??) in the system tray (the far right side) of the taskbar.

2 The **Date/Time Properties** dialog box appears. From the Date & Time tab, click the correct date on the calendar and the date will change. Choose the correct month from the drop down list box. After clicking the spin box, either type in or choose the correct year from the spin box. Also in a spin box control, you can edit each section of the Time. Make sure you remember to choose the AM or PM.

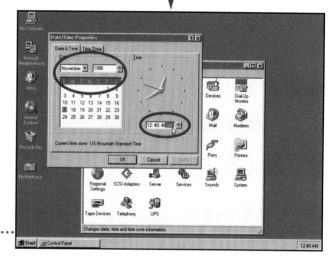

3 When you have finished entering the Date and Time, choose the **Time Zone** tab. This tab will allow you to choose the time zone that you reside in from a drop down list box. You can also select the check box to **Automatically update clock for daylight savings changes**. When you have finished selecting the appropriate time zone, you can either choose the **Apply** or **OK** buttons to see the changes in your system tray. If you choose **Apply**, you then need to choose **OK** to close the Date/time Properties dialog box. ■

Customizing the Desktop's Background

"Why would I do this?"

Many people like to personalize what their
desktop looks like. Some people choose a specific
wallpaper, create a pattern for themselves, or
even load scanned pictures of family members.
Whatever you choose, Windows NT makes it
easy to customize your desktop background.

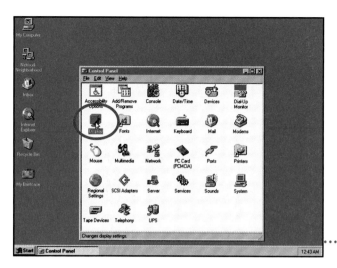

1 You should still have the Control Panel open. If not, from the **Start** menu, choose **Settings**, **Control Panel**. Double-click the **Display** icon.

> **Missing Link**
>
> A faster way to access the **Display Properties** dialog box is to right-click somewhere on a blank part of the desktop and choose **Properties** from the quick menu.

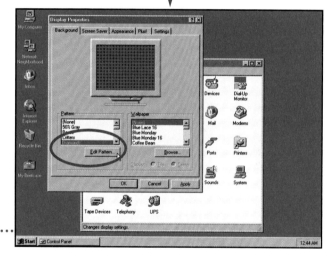

2 The **Display Properties** dialog box will appear. From the **Background** tab, choose any of the patterns from the **Pattern** list box. We are going to choose the **Diamonds** pattern. You can see the pattern in the example screen. Additionally, you can edit any of the patterns. Choose the **Edit Pattern** button.

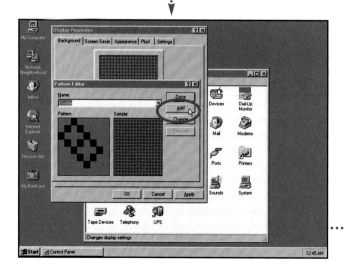

3 The **Pattern Editor** dialog box will appear. We want to make the Diamonds pattern into a double-diamond. See how the pattern has changed in the example screen. When finished, you can choose the **Done** button and save it to the original name (Diamonds), or give the pattern a new name (**Double**) and choose the **Add** button. An **Unsaved Pattern** message box will appear and ask you if you want to save your changes. Choose **Yes** if you do; choose **No** if you do not.

Task 69: Customizing the Desktop's Background

4 You will then be back at the **Display Properties** dialog box. Choose any of the patterns from the **Wallpaper** list box. We are going to choose the **Coffee Bean** wallpaper. You can see the wallpaper in the example screen.

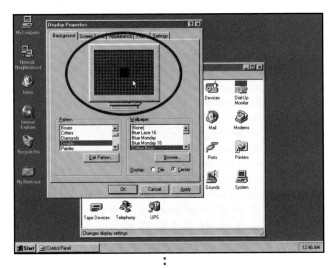

Missing Link

If you have wallpaper that you want to add to your computer, you can choose the **Browse** button. From the Browsing for wallpaper dialog box, select the file you want to be your wallpaper, and either double-click the file or choose the **Open** button.

5 When you have finished selecting the appropriate pattern and/or wallpaper, you can choose either the **Apply** or **OK** buttons to see the changes on your desktop. If you choose the **Cancel** button before you choose Apply, you will have made no changes. If you choose **Apply**, you then need to choose **OK** to accept the changes and close the Display Properties dialog box. ■

Missing Link

Images viewed in the Internet Explorer can also be used as wallpaper. To immediately use it as the wallpaper, right-click the image. From the context menu, choose the Set as Wallpaper command.

Changing Desktop Schemes

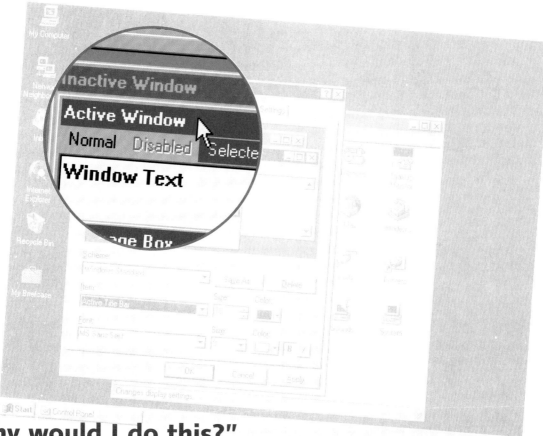

"Why would I do this?"

In addition to changing your desktop's background, you can change the scheme of your background (while keeping your pattern, wallpaper, or image), choose or create a new color for your desktop, or even alter the size and fonts of different desktop items like icons or Tooltips. Some people need high contrast combinations of colors due to visual problems, but many people just prefer colors of their own choice. Windows NT lets you make all these types of changes, quickly and easily.

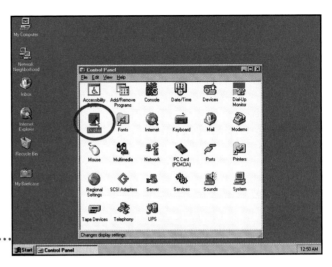

1 You should still have the Control Panel open. If not, from the **Start** menu, choose **Settings**, **Control Panel**. Double-click the **Display** icon.

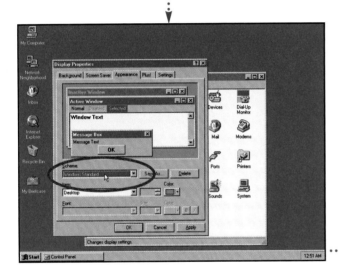

2 The **Display Properties** dialog box will appear. Choose the **Appearance** tab. (The default Scheme is Windows Standard.)

3 Choose any of the schemes from the **Scheme** list box. We have chosen the **Rose** scheme. Notice that the menus changed color, size, and font.

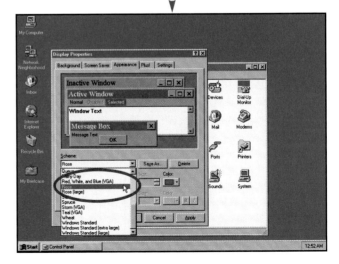

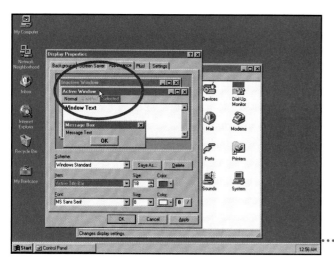

4 To alter any specific items on your desktop, you can click in the example display screen and the item will automatically show up in the **Item** and **Font** drop down list boxes. Then you will be able to change colors and fonts for each specific item.

5 We are going to choose the **Windows Standard** scheme, but alter the **Desktop** item to be a different color. Click the down arrow on the **Color** control. On the **Color** control, choose the **Other** button to create or choose a color. After you pick a color from the **Color** dialog box, choose the **OK** button to return back to the Appearance tab.

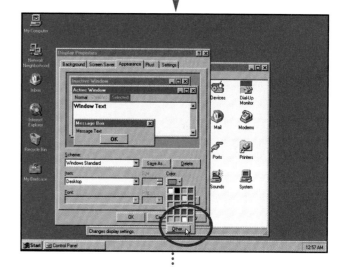

Missing Link

If you would like to delete any of the Windows NT schemes, choose the **Scheme** drop down list box and choose **Delete** to get rid of the item.

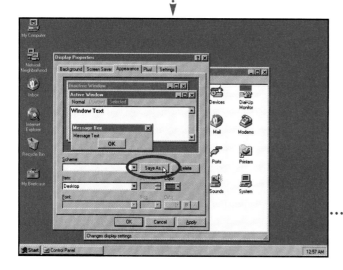

6 If you alter your desktop appearance and would like to save it as a specific scheme, choose the **Save As** button.

7 A **Save Scheme** dialog box will appear asking you what you want to name your scheme. Enter the specific name and choose the **OK** button. We are going to save ours as **Que**. If you decide you do not want to save a scheme, choose the **Cancel** button.

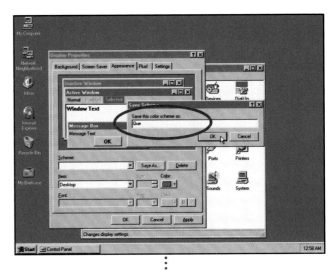

Puzzled?

If you modify an item that you did not want to change, you can choose the **Cancel** button on the **Display Properties** dialog box and none of your changes will apply.

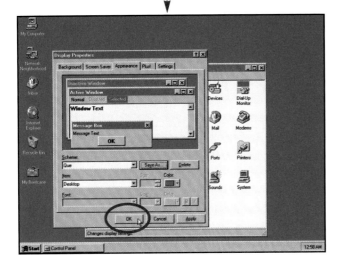

8 When you have finished selecting the appropriate scheme, colors and/or fonts, you can choose either the **Apply** or **OK** buttons to see the changes on your desktop. If you choose **Apply**, you then need to choose **OK** to accept the changes and close the **Display Properties** dialog box. ■

TASK

71

Changing Display Settings

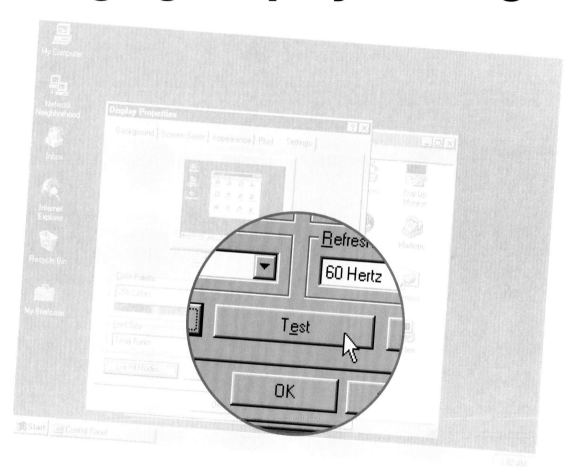

"Why would I do this?"

If you wanted to be able to fit more on your desktop, you might want to change the display settings. The most common display setting changed is the *resolution*, or desktop area. With the desktop area being made up by pixels, more of them lets you fit more on the screen. Conversely, less of these pixels fits less on the

screen. This can be translated to how your screen appears. More pixels means they are closer together, which makes the graphics seem clearer, items appear smaller (windows, icons, and so on), and allows for more room on the desktop for windows.

1 You should still have the Control Panel open. If not, from the **Start** menu, choose **Settings**, **Control Panel**. Double-click the **Display** icon.

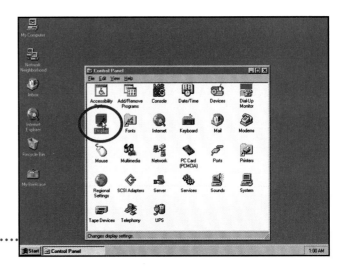

2 The **Display Properties** dialog box will appear. Choose the **Settings** tab. Before you can alter your desktop settings, you need to detect what mode your monitor will allow you to use. Choose the **List All Modes** button.

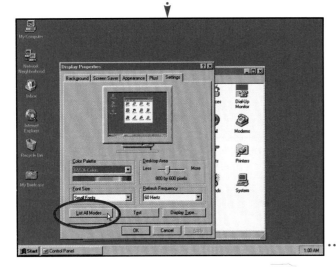

3 The **Detected Adapter** dialog box will appear and show you whether your monitor will allow for larger desktop settings. For now, if you have the option, choose **800 by 600 pixels, 256 Colors, 60 Hertz** and choose the **OK** button. Whatever you choose in this window, automatically changes your Settings tab.

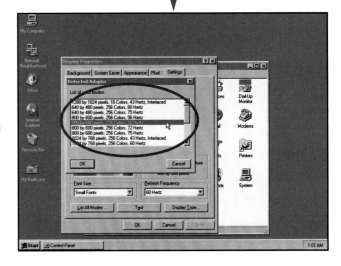

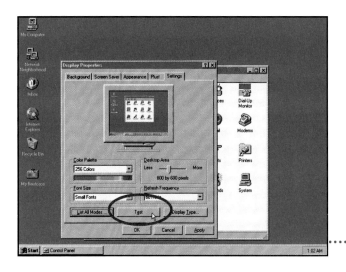

4 On the **Settings** tab, choose the **Test** button.

5 A **Testing Mode** message box will appear, letting you know that your monitor will be tested. Choose **OK**, then in five seconds, you will know if your monitor will accept the new mode. During that five seconds, your screen will go black and then a very colorful screen with Red, Green, Blue, Yellow, Magenta, Cyan, gradients, and lines will appear.

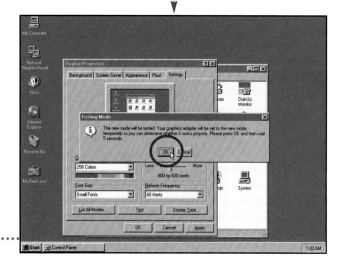

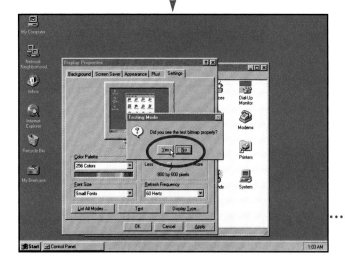

6 The **Testing Mode** message box will appear and ask you whether the bitmap test was correct. If you did get the colorful screen displayed correctly, choose **Yes**, and you will be returned to the Settings tab. From here, you can choose **OK** and your monitor will temporarily turn off and back on with the new settings displayed.

7 If you did not get the colorful screen displayed correctly, choose **No**. Another **Testing Mode** message box will appear, telling you why the test didn't work. Choose the **OK** button in this dialog box and you will be returned to the **Display Properties** dialog box. From here, choose the **Cancel** button and your old settings, that worked, will apply; or try different settings and test them. ▪

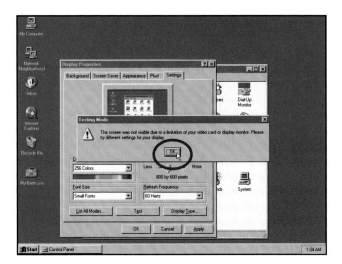

Using a Screen Saver

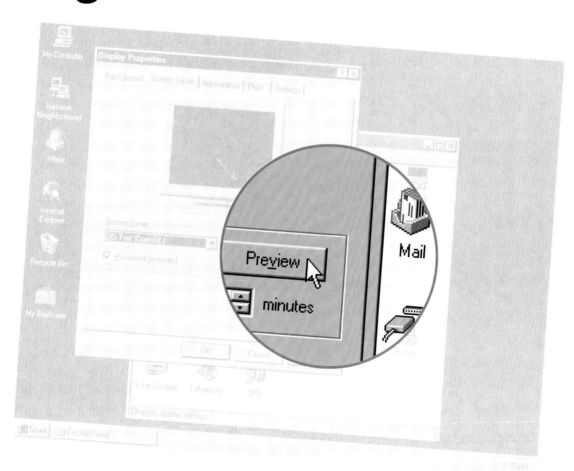

"Why would I do this?"

Monitors degrade with use, particularly when the same image is displayed continuously. Over time, these images "burn" into the screen phosphors, resulting in a *ghost* image. Though newer monitor screens take much longer to show the effects of ghosting, a screen saver is still recommended to change the screen display while you are away from your computer. In addition, you can assign a password to your screen saver that can keep passers-by from accessing your computer. Though, this type of password is not inaccessible, for better security, lock your workstation (See Task 4).

1 You should still have the **Control Panel** open. If not, from the **Start** menu, choose **Settings**, **Control Panel**. Double-click the **Display** icon.

Missing Link

A faster way to access the Display Properties dialog box is to right-click somewhere on a blank part of the desktop and choose **Properties** from the quick menu.

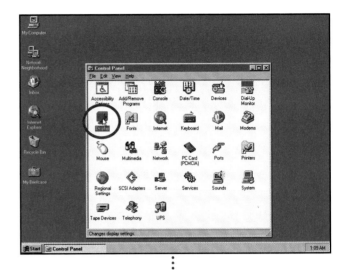

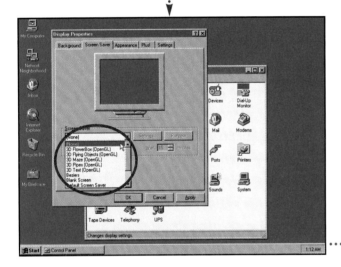

2 The **Display Properties** dialog box will appear. Choose the **Screen Saver** tab. Click the drop down list box arrow and choose from the many **Screen Savers**.

3 Pick the screen saver you like. For this example, we are going to choose the **3D Text (Open GL)** screen saver. You can choose to have your screen saver use your Windows NT password to restrict access to your session. You would check the **Password protected** check box. In the **Wait** list box, you can set your screen saver to come on when your computer has been idle for a specific time period. Now choose the **Settings** button.

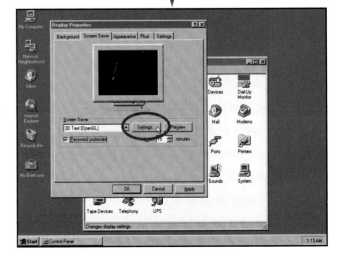

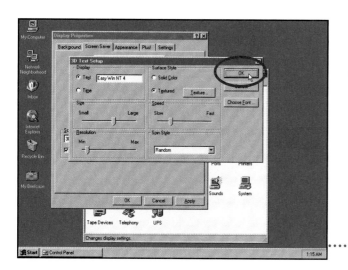

4 The **3D Text Setup** dialog box will appear. You can put in **Display** text up to sixteen characters or the time. You can change the **Surface Style**, **Size**, **Speed**, **Resolution**, **Spin Style**, and **Font** of your text. When you have altered the settings to your liking, choose the **OK** button and you will be back at the Screensaver tab.

5 To preview your changes, either watch the screen example or choose the **Preview** button. The screen saver will appear on your entire screen until you press a key on the keyboard or move the mouse. When you are satisfied with the changes to your screen saver, choose **OK** in the Display Properties dialog box. ■

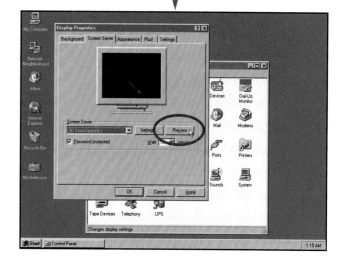

Missing Link

If you want the surface style of your screen saver text to be textured, choose the **Texture** button and choose one by double-clicking the filename in the **Choose Texture File** dialog box. In addition, you can have a texture on disk and load that file. If you want to pick a particular font, choose the **Choose Font** button and from the Font dialog box, click the font you want and choose the **OK** button.

Adjusting the Mouse

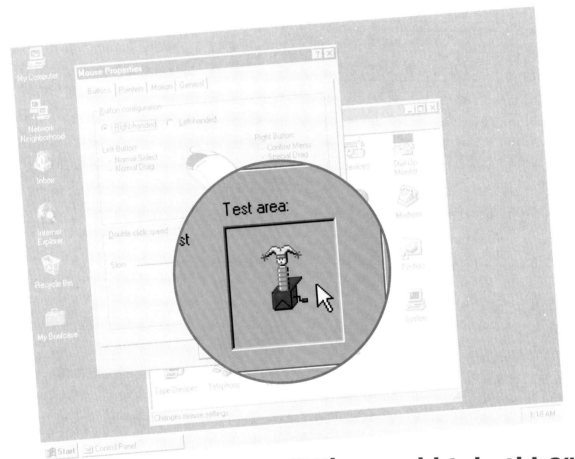

"Why would I do this?"

When you first use the mouse with Windows NT, you might want the settings to be slow because you are still learning. Once you have become more familiar with using the mouse and Windows NT, you will probably want to speed up the mouse to help you work more efficiently. This task will show you how to adjust your mouse properties.

1 You should still have the Control Panel open. If not, from the **Start** menu, choose **Settings**, **Control Panel**. Double-click the **Mouse** icon.

2 The **Mouse Properties** dialog box will appear. From the **Buttons** tab, select the **Button configuration** that is appropriate for you. Choose the **Right-handed** or **Left-handed** radio buttons.

Puzzled?

Switching the right and left-handed mouse buttons will make the normal select (click) and drag switch from the left button, on the right button. The context menu and special drag from the right button, will switch to the left button.

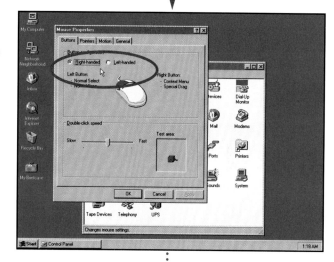

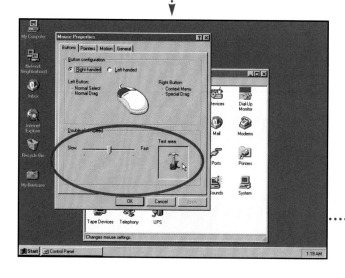

3 In the lower portion of the **Buttons** tab is the **Double-click speed** section. You can test the double-click speed of your mouse. Move the slider bar towards the **Fast** side and double-click in the **Test** area. If the jack-in-the-box emerges or disappears, your double-click was recognized, thus an appropriate speed. If it does not, you might need to move the slider bar towards the **Slow** side and try again.

231

4 Choose the **Pointers** tab to change the appearance of a pointer. You can choose a scheme from the **Scheme** drop down list box. All the pointers will change according to the scheme. Or, you can select a specific pointer from the large list box, choose the **Browse** button, and double-click specific cursors from the **Browse** dialog box.

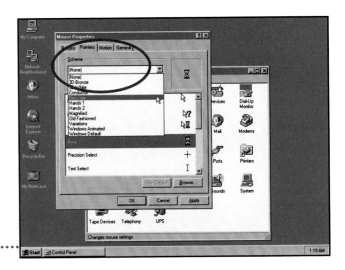

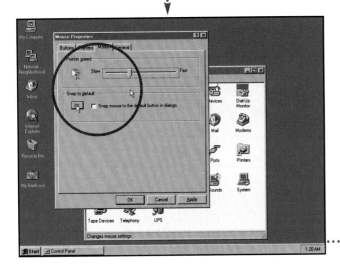

5 Choose the **Motion** tab to change your pointer speed. Adjust the option by moving the slider bar between the **Slow** and **Fast Pointer speed**. **Snap to default** indicates whether the mouse pointer will snap to the default button (such as OK or Apply) in dialog boxes. Choose the check box if you want this feature.

6 If you buy a new or different mouse for your computer, choose the **General** tab, choose the **Change** button, and follow the directions on-screen. When you have finished selecting the mouse settings, you can either choose the **Apply** or **OK** buttons to try the changes on your desktop. If you choose **Apply**, you then need to choose **OK** to close the Mouse Properties dialog box. ■

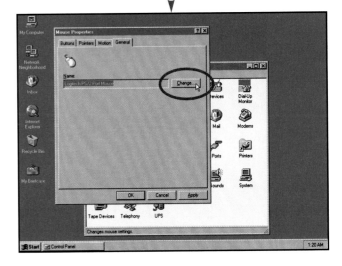

Adding Fonts

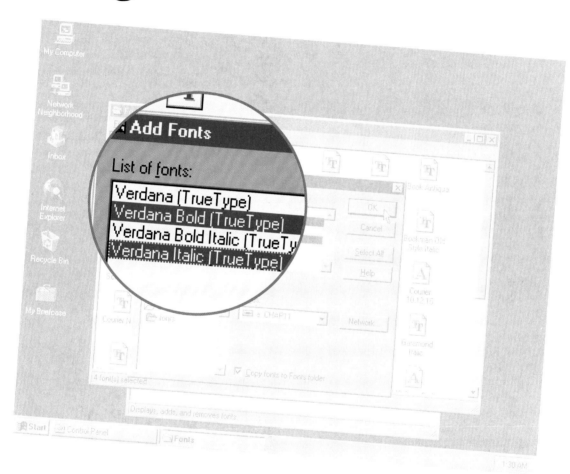

"Why would I do this?"

You can add a variety of fonts to Windows NT and then use them in any of your Windows NT applications. There are many fonts available that will help make your documents look attractive and professional.

1 You should still have the Control Panel open. If not, from the **Start** menu, choose **Settings**, **Control Panel**. Double-click the **Fonts** icon.

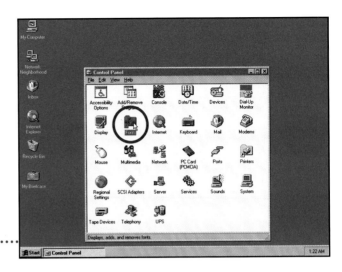

2 The **Fonts** window will appear. From the **File** menu, choose the **Install New Fonts** command.

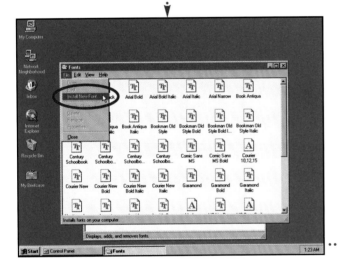

3 The **Add Fonts** dialog box appears. In the **Drives** drop down list box, choose the drive in which the fonts you want to install are located. Windows NT changes drives and lists the available fonts in the **List of Fonts** box.

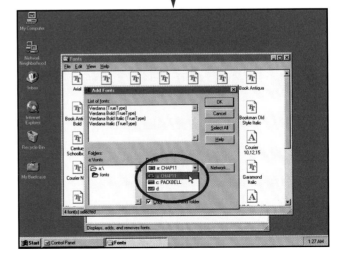

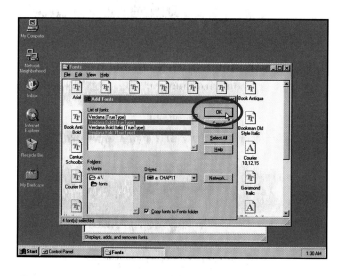

4 Select the font(s) you want to install or choose the **Select All** button if you want to install all the fonts on the disk. Choose the **OK** button in the Add Fonts dialog box. Windows NT copies the fonts to the Windows NT fonts folder and adds the **Close** to the Fonts dialog box list. Close the Fonts window by choosing the **(X)** button. ■

Missing Link

You can select successive files by holding down the **Shift** key and clicking the files you want. You can also select specific files (non-successive) by holding the **Ctrl** key and clicking the files you want.

Puzzled?

TrueType fonts use the TTF extension, this makes them easy to identify. You can also install font files with a FON or FOT extension, and others.

Changing the Taskbar

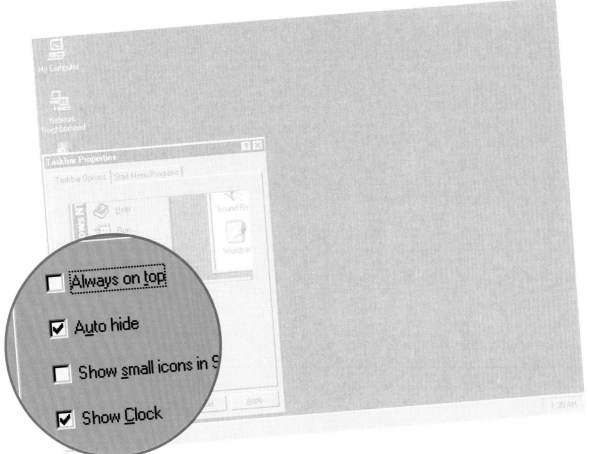

"Why would I do this?"

You can personalize the taskbar, just like many other settings in Windows NT. The taskbar is displayed at the bottom of your Windows NT desktop. This is where you access the Start menu, view the clock in the system tray, and can switch between files, folders, and applications.

1 Open the **Start** menu and choose **Settings**. A secondary menu appears. From the secondary menu, choose **Taskbar**.

Missing Link

Another way to access the Taskbar Properties dialog box, is to right click the taskbar and select **Properties** from the quick menu.

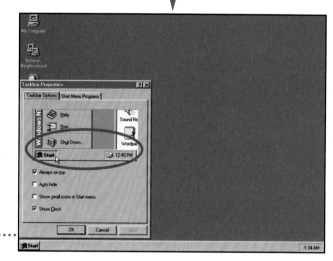

2 From the **Taskbar Properties** dialog box, notice the display screen in the **Taskbar Options** tab. You can see what your current desktop looks like when you select the **Start** menu.

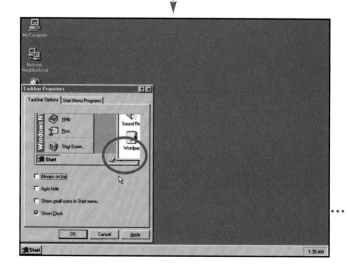

3 The taskbar default is to be in front of any window on the desktop. If you deselect the **Always on top** check box, you can see the difference in the display screen. Other windows will be able to cover up the taskbar.

237

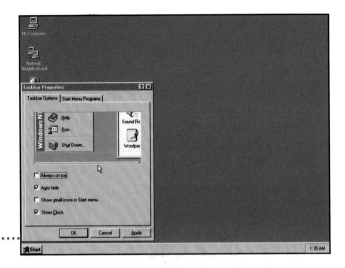

4 The taskbar will always be visible at the bottom of your desktop. If you have selected the **Auto hide** check box, you can see the difference in the display screen. The taskbar will then only be visible when you move your mouse to the bottom of the desktop, where the taskbar would be.

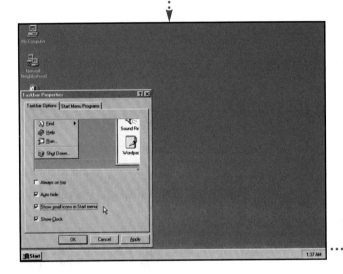

5 Large icons will be the default on your Start menu. If you select the **Show small icons in Start menu** check box, you can see the difference in the display screen. The icons are smaller.

6 Another taskbar default is to display the clock in the right corner of the system tray. If you deselect the **Show Clock** check box, you can see the difference in the display screen. The clock will not be displayed. When you have finished selecting the taskbar properties, you can either choose the **Apply** or **OK** buttons to try the changes on your desktop. If you choose **Apply**, you then need to choose **OK** to close the Taskbar Properties dialog box. ■

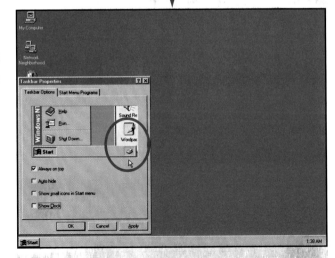

Index

symbols

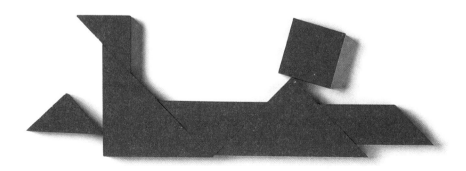

Index

MACMILLAN COMPUTER PUBLISHING USA

A VIACOM COMPANY

Technical ---- **Support:**

If you need assistance with the information in this book or with a CD/Disk accompanying the book, please access the Knowledge Base on our Web site at **http://www.superlibrary.com/general/support**. Our most Frequently Asked Questions are answered there. If you do not find the answer to your questions on our Web site, you may contact Macmillan Technical Support **(317) 581-3833** or e-mail us at **support@mcp.com**.

Complete and Return this Card
for a *FREE* Computer Book Catalog

Thank you for purchasing this book! You have purchased a superior computer book written expressly for your needs. To continue to provide the kind of up-to-date, pertinent coverage you've come to expect from us, we need to hear from you. Please take a minute to complete and return this self-addressed, postage-paid form. In return, we'll send you a free catalog of all our computer books on topics ranging from word processing to programming and the internet.

Mr. ☐   Mrs. ☐   Ms. ☐   Dr. ☐

Name (first) ☐☐☐☐☐☐☐☐   (M.I.) ☐   (last) ☐☐☐☐☐☐☐☐☐☐☐☐☐☐☐

Address ☐☐☐☐☐☐☐☐☐☐☐☐☐☐☐☐☐☐☐☐☐☐☐☐☐☐☐☐☐☐☐☐☐☐☐

☐☐☐☐☐☐☐☐☐☐☐☐☐☐☐☐☐☐☐☐☐☐☐☐☐☐☐☐☐☐☐☐☐☐☐

City ☐☐☐☐☐☐☐☐☐☐☐☐☐☐☐   State ☐☐   Zip ☐☐☐☐☐ ☐☐☐☐

Phone ☐☐☐ ☐☐☐☐ ☐☐☐☐   Fax ☐☐☐ ☐☐☐☐ ☐☐☐☐

Company Name ☐☐☐☐☐☐☐☐☐☐☐☐☐☐☐☐☐☐☐☐☐☐☐☐☐☐☐☐☐☐☐

E-mail address ☐☐☐☐☐☐☐☐☐☐☐☐☐☐☐☐☐☐☐☐☐☐☐☐☐☐☐☐☐

1. Please check at least (3) influencing factors for purchasing this book.

Front or back cover information on book .... ☐
Special approach to the content .... ☐
Completeness of content .... ☐
Author's reputation .... ☐
Publisher's reputation .... ☐
Book cover design or layout .... ☐
Index or table of contents of book .... ☐
Price of book .... ☐
Special effects, graphics, illustrations .... ☐
Other (Please specify): _____ ☐

2. How did you first learn about this book?

Saw in Macmillan Computer Publishing catalog .... ☐
Recommended by store personnel .... ☐
Saw the book on bookshelf at store .... ☐
Recommended by a friend .... ☐
Received advertisement in the mail .... ☐
Saw an advertisement in: _____ ☐
Read book review in: _____ ☐
Other (Please specify): _____ ☐

3. How many computer books have you purchased in the last six months?

This book only .... ☐   3 to 5 books .... ☐
2 books .... ☐   More than 5 .... ☐

4. Where did you purchase this book?

Bookstore .... ☐
Computer Store .... ☐
Consumer Electronics Store .... ☐
Department Store .... ☐
Office Club .... ☐
Warehouse Club .... ☐
Mail Order .... ☐
Direct from Publisher .... ☐
Internet site .... ☐
Other (Please specify): _____ ☐

5. How long have you been using a computer?

☐ Less than 6 months   ☐ 6 months to a year
☐ 1 to 3 years   ☐ More than 3 years

6. What is your level of experience with personal computers and with the subject of this book?

	With PCs	With subject of book
New	☐	☐
Casual	☐	☐
Accomplished	☐	☐
Expert	☐	☐

Source Code ISBN: 0-7897-1164-8

7. Which of the following best describes your job title?

Administrative Assistant .... ☐
Coordinator .... ☐
Manager/Supervisor .... ☐
Director .... ☐
Vice President .... ☐
President/CEO/COO .... ☐
Lawyer/Doctor/Medical Professional .... ☐
Teacher/Educator/Trainer .... ☐
Engineer/Technician .... ☐
Consultant .... ☐
Not employed/Student/Retired .... ☐
Other (Please specify): _____ ☐

8. Which of the following best describes the area of the company your job title falls under?

Accounting .... ☐
Engineering .... ☐
Manufacturing .... ☐
Operations .... ☐
Marketing .... ☐
Sales .... ☐
Other (Please specify): _____ ☐

●●●

Comments: _____
_____
_____

9. What is your age?

Under 20 .... ☐
21-29 .... ☐
30-39 .... ☐
40-49 .... ☐
50-59 .... ☐
60-over .... ☐

10. Are you:

Male .... ☐
Female .... ☐

11. Which computer publications do you read regularly? (Please list)

_____
_____
_____
_____
_____
_____
_____
_____
_____
_____

Fold here and scotch-tape to mail.